Music in American Society
1776-1976

Music in American Society 1776-1976

From Puritan Hymn to Synthesizer

Edited by
George McCue

Transaction Books
New Brunswick, New Jersey

Library of Congress Catalog Number: 76-24527.
ISBN: 0-87855-209-X(cloth); 0-87855-634-7(paper).
Printed in the United States of America.

Library of Congress Cataloging in Publication Data
Main entry under title:

Music in American society 1776-1976.

    Includes index.
    CONTENTS: Schuman, W. Americanism in music, a composer's view.–Jablonski, E. Music with an American accent.–Caswell, A. B. Social and moral music, the hymn. [etc.]
    1. Music, American–Addresses, essays, lectures. I. McCue, George.
ML200.1.M9   781.7'73   76-24527
ISBN 0-87855-209-X
ISBN 0-87855-634-7 pbk.

Contents

Acknowledgments

Acknowledgment is gratefully given to the following publishers for permission to reprint their material in chapter 4, "Charles Ives's Optimism: or, The Program's Progress," by Roy V. Magers.

To Associated Music Publishers for quotations from Henry Bellamann's 1927 program notes to the Charles Ives *Symphony no. 4*, which appears in John Kirkpatrick's Preface to the published score.

To W. W. Norton for quotations from *Essays Before a Sonata, The Majority, and Other Writings* by Charles Ives, edited by Howard Boatwright (1970).

To Peer International Corporation for the quotation from the Introduction to "Romanzo di Central Park" from *Fourteen Songs* by Charles Ives (1955):
Copyright © 1955 by Peer International Corporation; used by permission.

To Theodore Presser Company for quotations from "Majority" and "The Innate" from *Nineteen Songs* by Charles Ives (Merion Music, Inc./Theodore Presser Co., 1935).

Preface

This book is the literary legacy of a national music festival in St. Louis, organized to identify as clearly as possible the specifically native character of music originating in the United States of America. The festival—the Bicentennial Horizons of American Music and the Performing Arts (B.H.A.M.)—sponsored more than 250 performances and workshops between Flag Day and Independence Day 1976. It was the only event of the Bicentennial celebration to address itself to a survey and evaluation of the musical development of this country.

During the festival's three weeks, the St. Louis community resounded to the music of bands, groups, orchestras, choruses, instrumental and vocal soloists, recordings made by field researchers, and music from electronic systems. The music was performed on the Mississippi River levee under the great Gateway Arch, in Powell Symphony Hall, in academic halls and classrooms, in widely dispersed municipal and county parks, in the streets of downtown St. Louis, and in television and radio broadcasts. These events provided exposure to the gamut of music and musical ideas developed during this country's two centuries as a nation, and in the prior century and a half as a cluster of English colonies, and French and Spanish settlements.

The one event designed to bring the festival's purpose into historical and philosophical focus was a symposium of twelve musicians and musicologists, each an authority of high reputation. All took part in workshops and discussions at twelve participating universities and colleges, and other BHAM events, but they did not assemble all together at any one time. Their platform is this book, and their symposium takes place here, in these pages, in papers that in most cases were prepared for this publication rather than for workshop use. The contributors were explicitly concerned with the American character in music, not as a mannerism but rather, in the words of William Schuman, as "simply feeling the national spirit and breathing with it, however loosely or vaguely that may be defined." They have undertaken to survey the exceedingly diverse American style and sound from all segments of American society—from rural, urban, and ethnic sources, with their relation to the corporate, governmental, commercial, and private sectors that have become increasingly influential in supporting and giving direction to this country's creative talent.

The idea for the symposium/book was advanced by K. Peter Etzkorn, of the University of Missouri, St. Louis, who became one of the contributors. He was joined in its planning by Dr. Allen C. Larson, associate professor of music, Webster College, and by Frank Peters, music critic of the St. Louis *Post-Dispatch*, also a contributor. The project was guided through many a crisis by the resourcefulness and never-failing good humor of the festival chairman, Elizabeth Gentry (Mrs. Homer E.) Sayad.

Among innumerable obligations, special thanks are owed to Frances Gillett, professor of music, St. Louis Community College at Meramec; Constance Smith, head of acquisitions, Pius XII Library, St. Louis University; and the Rev. Francis J. Guentner, S.J., professor of music, St. Louis University, for research assistance. Financial support of the Missouri State Council on the Arts and the participating universities and colleges is gratefully acknowledged. BHAM was sponsored by the St. Louis Spirit of '76 and cosponsored by the National Park Service.

The term *American* is used here with recognition that it properly refers to any and all of the nations of the Western Hemisphere. An acceptable national adjectival reference to the United States of America has not yet been devised, and there is no choice but to employ "American" with this special application.

Music in American Society
1776-1976

1

Americanism in Music: A Composer's View

William Schuman

This volume supplies a number of scholarly inquiries into various categories and aspects of American music, written by respected specialists. My assignment is different from theirs, and is quite specific: I am asked to write an introduction to this printed symposium on music in American society, from the perspective of a practicing composer—one who is identified as an *American* composer, who takes satisfaction in being so identified, and who might therefore conceivably make some contribution toward a definition of the "American" character in our music. At this late date, our country's two hundredth birthday, one might wonder why it should seem necessary to attempt to define (or to redefine) the characteristics that make American music American, yet even now the undertaking is not a simple one: there are many questions to be asked, and more than a few allow for a plurality of valid answers.

We can, however, at least proceed from the acknowledgment that there *is* a more or less generally recognizable American character in music, as distinctive in its way—or ways—as the music, say, of Spain, Russia, France, or Scandinavia. In all these countries, as it is in our own, there have been movements to encourage native composers to create music in a "national" style, and, possibly more significant, many of them have produced such music entirely spontaneously, without the need for such encouragement and without self-consciousness. A great deal of music has been produced by now, in our country as well as elsewhere, that unarguably exudes the pulse and flavor of the land and its people, and this has not so much to do with the use of folk material, or writing in a folk style, as with simply feeling the national spirit and breathing with it, however loosely or vaguely that may be defined.

Some of the more obvious questions that come to mind are: What are the attitudes and approaches toward Americanism in music that apply specifically to composers? Do composers think, when they want to write music, that in this or that particular work they wish to be "American"? Is the process a conscious one? Is there some special thinking, some special intellectual or emotional adjustment, that goes into the writing of works that are supposed to be "American"? Is the process different from writing abstract works that are not given nationalistic titles? Is there special conditioning or preparation required, or is the identity something as natural as our various regional speech-patterns? Different composers may answer some or all of these questions differently; I think the best way for me to deal with them is to speak for myself and not attempt to present a consensus. My comments, moreover, will only relate to some of the criteria inherent in considering these and similar questions rather than attempting to supply authoritative answers. And, too, I should like to add that we are really talking about United States music since the term *American* includes countries other than our own.

When a piece of music draws the comment, "Only an American could have composed that," the meaning is far from precise: what is "American" in American music is only peripherally (if at all) measurable by the criteria of scholarly investigation. It has, as I have suggested, more to do with feeling. These Americanisms spring from a complex of factors, largely of emotional recollection, for the qualities that make music identifiably American are, to a large degree if not basically, in the ear of the beholder. When enough beholders perceive the product to be indigenous, then so it becomes. A body of recognizable characteristics has emerged through the collective experience of listeners over a long period of time, and we call the result *American*. However, since listeners are as varied in their sophistication as the extraordinary range of American music itself, the inexact nature of these characteristics becomes the more apparent when we attempt to pinpoint or define them in terms of universals.

We do not even ask this question—"Is American music truly American?"—about all categories of music. We ask it only about what we might call *formal music*, the music of the established concert and theater categories, while the Americanism of most American music is taken for granted. We assume, for example, that the marches of Sousa are as thoroughly American as the waltzes of Strauss are thoroughly Viennese, and the thought of asking whether they are would simply never occur to us. Why, to articulate such an inquiry about Sousa's marches would be foolish, gratuitous, and even, I suppose, un-American! In the same way, we never ponder the authenticity of the Americanism of what we hear in any form of popular music, whatever the category; if we are told that the music really came from distant lands, which were the founding sources of some of our most treasured popular music, it is of little interest except perhaps to scholars. The whole wealth of our nonformal music, then, is by use, tradition, and long affection *ours*, unmistakably in the American tradition regardless of the original sources. It has become genuinely Americanized through indigenous use, our expression as a people in all our incredible and fascinating variety.

From my point of view then, as an individual composer, I am not attempting to comment upon the many categories of music dealt with in the chapters that follow, but limit my observations to so-called serious or concert music, and even more specifically to the symphonic.

Only a chauvinist would claim there is a qualitative factor related to Americanism in music—that is, that the degree of identifiable "Americanism" in a work directly affects or indicates its value. Whether or not a piece is "Americana" has nothing to do with its being a better or less good musical work. Yet I think a distinction must be made between commentators, on one hand, who say that locale has absolutely no importance —that is, where one happens to live when one writes a piece of music makes no difference in his writing of it—and critics who claim a qualitative aspect measured in terms of whether a work is "American" or not. My own feeling is that if a work sounds American to us, then we have a most intriguing special category of music, music that relates our own American composers to their native soil in the same way composers of such countries as Britain, Italy, and Spain are related to theirs. Since nationalism, or patriotism, can give music a special flavor but cannot alone ever ensure its quality, works that are American in orientation are neither better nor worse for that reason than music composed in an international style—that is, a style that could have come from any composer anywhere in the world, granted a similar ambience.

If we agree, then, that a recognizable national character in music in itself carries no particular merit, is this question really of any importance? The answer is assuredly *Yes.* Traits do emerge. Localities, from small units to large, engender particularities, be they of dress, cuisine, gesture, attitudes, or a thousand other categories. It is the particularity of American symphonic music that I believe can be recognized and, perhaps to some degree, demonstrated to prove that we do have an American music. And this national connection, it seems to me, is more than just the comfort of belonging, of local identification: it can represent a genuine and deep-felt need on the part of both composer and listener.

It is not that we need to prove there is musical life here, heaven knows, for in our century the United States has become both an export and import nation of prime importance in music. In the nineteenth century we certainly did not export our performing artists on any meaningful scale, and did not import musicians who would come to these shores for their training. What little importing and exporting we did then were in the obverse of that pattern: a few virtuosi imported to perform, a few serious students exported to study in Europe. All that has changed dramatically now. American performing artists are in demand the world over, and our professional music education has reached such a high point of development that serious students now come from the old centers of learning in Europe as well as from everywhere else in the world to study here.

But performing and education alone, however excellent, while validating an intensity of musical activity, obviously do not make for the culture of a country. It is the creative artist who gives the country its stamp as a mature nation in terms of any art; in music we have, over the past fifty years or so especially, developed our own composers and our own school of composition, which certainly stand on a level with that of any other country in the world. I do not mean to minimize or dismiss the efforts and estimable accomplishments of composers in the United States before the twentieth century, but it is surely in the last half century that we have seen the maturation of American creativity in music, the flowering of the American school.

In music, as it is in the other arts, the creative artist's intention to strive consciously for expression of his locale, or consciously to avoid such expression, or to ignore that consideration altogether, need not, and ought not, be a major factor; personally, I think it is wholly beside the point of genuine creative motivation. The real point is simply that for some creators there is such a oneness between their own work and their origin that this oneness often has to be expressed in a straightforward, identifiable way that is wholly natural, wholly uncontrived. This is the need I alluded to a few paragraphs back: whether consciously felt or not, I believe it accounts for much of the music that is nationalistic in spirit. Here again, while I must emphasize that this national or local identification has nothing to do with superficial flag-waving or chauvinism, and that it also, no matter how deeply felt, is neither assurance nor measurement of musical worth, it does constitute an extra element of direct communication.

The formative environments in which artists grow naturally and inevitably have enormous impact on the work the artists produce. It is equally true that these impacts need not necessarily be revealed through localized emphasis. As noted above, for some creators this sense of identification, and the need to express it, are fundamental and essential parts of their natural creative process. This applies, of course, not only to American composers, but also to composers, poets, painters, and other creative artists in all cultures.

It is reasonable at this point, then, to ask: What is an American composer? A simple answer often given is that an American composer is one who is born in the United States, or one who is a citizen of the United States, or one who has come to this country and spent his formative years here. For example, one could never rightly claim a Hindemith or a Stravinsky or a Schoenberg as American, since these composers' formative years were not spent here and obviously their work is not identifiably American (though Hindemith, who spent the least time here, did succeed to some degree through the words of Walt Whitman in capturing an American flavor in his requiem, *When Lilacs Last in the Dooryard Bloom'd*). On the other hand, there are composers who have come from distant shores who have spent their formative years here, and may or may not have developed into composers we recognize as American in terms of the character of their music. Indeed, then, this question might be answered in two ways: American composers are individuals who write music that we feel is American in approach and sound, and people who happen to be Americans but who produce music that is not identifiable in terms of a national character.

A step beyond this in dealing with this question might be the establishment of two sets of criteria for determining "Americanism" in music. The first would be a set of general descriptions—adjectives—with which we attempt to define specifically American qualities; the second would be an examination to determine whether there are any measurable techniques connected with American music that might give us a bit more to go on than pure speculation.

One often hears that American music is optimistic (affirmative is the interchangeable term), or typically sentimental, or that it reflects the quality of jazz. But surely if we talk about optimism, or poignancy, or pessimism, or large-scale or small-grain, or even the jazz influence in particular, we are using descriptive phrases that could be applied to many different kinds of music being written in many different lands. We would have to go much farther than this to arrive at any sort of convincing definition by means of adjectives. If we say that this music could only have been written by a man who understood the vastness of the plains, then we might well ask what is so different about the vastness of the plains in America in contradistinction to the steppes in Russia, for example, in terms of inspiration for a large-scale, broad utterance. If we speak of introspective music, that is surely to be found in the works of composers of every land and every period. No, if these adjectives are to be at all helpful in defining American music, then they themselves must be further defined, beyond their broader applicability.

When we come to the use of popular idioms—jazz in particular—and say there are typical rhythms or melodic turns or orchestral devices, then we begin to approach something that has a little more substance in helping us reach a definition. In my view, one of the common threads running through all American music is the nature of its orchestration. That is, in broader terms, the actual sound of the instrumental speech through which the musical ideas are projected and communicated. I can think of no composer who is generally regarded as a creator of "American" music who is not a brilliant orchestrator.

I use the word *brilliant* here not merely in the sense of virtuosic skill, but in that of a specifically American kind of brilliance that I think is common to the music of all our best composers. If one examines the intrumental techniques of our leading composers, I believe a certain virtuosic manner will be observed that goes back very much to the extraordinary ability of our popular music performers and at the same time relates directly to the fantastic level of our American symphony orchestras. (Again, it is not that there are not great orchestras in other parts of the world, but the leading American orchestras are by now acknowledged to have set an overall level that exceeds most previously known standards.) Our composers who have grown up in the last fifty years have taken this virtuosity for granted and tend to be both daring and exuberantly confident in their orchestration. It might be revealing for some scholar to undertake a comparison of the specifics of orchestration among American composers in the last fifty years with those among European composers of the same period. I would not expect qualitative differences to emerge, for in general superior composers are superior orchestrators, but I think we might see a special kind of feeling for the orchestra—certain timbres, balances, colors—that might be identified as American.

In regard to my own music, it has always been rather difficult for me to differentiate between works that are said to be readily identifiable as American and the others since I feel no separation. For this reason it has seemed odd to me that some of my compositions have been labeled as "unmistakably American" and that the same has not been said of all my music. The answer, I think, is no more complex than the matter of titles. I recently saw a reference to a work by the late English composer Cyril Scott called *Tallahassee*. I presume the Tallahassee referred to is the capital city of Florida; I do not know this, nor have I ever heard the work or seen the score, but I feel safe in saying that the music will not sound American simply because it is called *Tallahassee,* any more than Dvorak's symphony will sound American because it is called *From the New World.* (A program note I happened to read recently suggested that Dvorak's symphony, still probably the most popular work composed in this country, is American to about the same degree that Gershwin's *An American in Paris* is French.) But there is something about the title of such a work that does predispose evaluators to refer to it as *American,* or as *more American* than pieces that might be given abstract or generic titles, or pieces that might be abstractions except for their descriptive titles. (This sort of thing is nothing new, of course: one only has to recall Robert Schumann's exclaiming over Mendelssohn's *Scotch Symphony,* which he mistook for the *Italian,* that it gave so fine a picture of Italy as to compensate the listener for never having visited there. We can never underestimate the suggestive power of titles.)

Aaron Copland has recalled that when he was a young man he was fascinated by French music (Debussy and Ravel were still writing in his youth, and Debussy was signing himself "musicien français"), and was taken especially by the idea that the French were writing French music, and that all music did not have to sound German. He thought then how wonderful it would be if there could be some recognizably American music. (Ives, we have to remember, was hardly a celebrated figure, nor his music at all well known, until after his death in 1954.) Of course, in following Copland and Roy Harris by a decade and more, I had the advantage of hearing what they were doing as I developed, so it never occurred to me to be consciously American. I simply took it for granted, as Copland himself wrote, that "when our music is mature it will also be American in quality. American individuals will produce an American music, without any help from conscious Americanisms." I think this prophecy has been fulfilled, and that its fulfillment continues.

The characteristics by now recognized as American are simply traits developed and shared by our strongest composers, the ones whose personal idioms reflect America to its people just as the characteristics of what the world knows as Finnish music are manifest in the personal idiom of Sibelius. As for Copland himself, I must say that, to me, his music is just as "American" in the *Third Symphony* as in *A Lincoln Portrait.* One assumes, of course, that the *Lincoln Portrait* is "American" because of its use of folk tunes and other Americanisms, and because of the specific nature of the work, while the symphony has no illustrative title nor declared programmatic significance. But the question is not whether the *Third Symphony* could have been written by anyone but an American. The point in question is that it could have been written by no one but Copland, who proclaims himself in that work, no less than in *Billy the Kid,* an American composer.

Now in the 1970s we seem less interested in writing music that is demonstrably American—perhaps because we have made the point effectively enough a hundred times over that Americans do write American music. In any event, that definition, and even an approach to it, remain to be pinned down. Do we fall back on the adjectival approach, or are there truly objective ways of looking at music and deciding what its American characteristics are? It still seems to me more a matter of feeling than of measurable criteria. When a composer writes music that is regarded as native or national, it follows that he has struck a responsive chord in his listeners, and that they recognize qualities that go back to their own sense of identification with their own land or culture. This is a wonderful thing for a composer to be able to do, and I think this has been achieved in American music despite the fact that the Americanisms, really, are very difficult to analyze or codify. I believe the important factor is that we now have a symphonic output by American composers that is truly exceptional in its range and its quality as well as quantity, and that much of this music does have the power to evoke shared inheritances.

What we still do not have, however, on the part of symphony orchestras and all but a handful of conductors is the conviction to support presentations of American music systematically and consistently. One can only hope that in the decades ahead this situation will improve, for if it does not our musical culture will continue to lack its fundamental attribute. I remarked earlier that a country is really cultured only if it has its own indigenous art; it remains, then, for our American music to be developed into a repertory. There are many individual works that are performed with great frequency but, in my view, we shall not really have an American repertory until we have every American symphony orchestra using American music as the mainstay of every season's programming. Not just an occasional token piece here or there, but the systematic building up of an identifiable and familiar list of American works and composers.

This need not—and certainly ought not—be done at the expense of the great masterworks of the past, nor of other contemporary music. The worst thing that could happen would be the narrow, parochial approach, the performing of American music just because it is American; I cannot believe any serious artist would ever wish this to happen. At the same time, I do not hesitate to raise the question of national pride.

It is difficult to imagine any other country in the world in which the orchestras would not rise to the riches of their own literature; it is really only in America that we have this kind of inverse chauvinism in which we are so often guilty of profligate neglect. My hope is that, having proved there is an American repertory, we shall continue to add to it by welcoming new composers, while not forgetting the music of the past, and that we shall build and continue to program those works that have won audiences. The most appalling waste is that we do have American symphonic works that have demonstrated their direct appeal to and success with audiences, and yet we tend to neglect even these.

Regarding our activity in the arts, one of the basic elements of our American character seems to be this "inverse chauvinism." We still constantly doubt, probe, question our own worth, ponder whether what we do is equal to the achievements of our European cousins. Self-criticism, in perspective, is almost always a good thing, but excessive humility can be crippling. Obviously, we have come of age musically in the United States, and need no longer question that fact. Our performers are superb, our educational resources are the finest anywhere, and on the creative level we can point to the extraordinary achievements of our composers, which we ourselves, ironically enough, may be the slowest to acknowledge.

The focus of this introduction, as stated, has been to comment on one particular aspect of Americanism in music through a consideration of some of the criteria germane to its definition. I warned that authoritative answers would not be forthcoming, and in this regard the reader has been faithfully served. The essays that follow treat other particulars in the rich fabric of our nation's music. It is the sum of all these particularities that can give us the generalities—the overview of the place of music in our lives, a place that when fully investigated supplies a fascinating and remarkably reliable vision of what we are.

2

Music with an American Accent

Edward Jablonski

There is a large body of musical Americana, rooted in song and dance (is not all music?), too often patronized under the heading of "light music," and generally relegated to summer concerts when, it might be presumed, "heavy music" is beyond the comprehension of the average languid listener. The summer "pops" purvey a stream of "semiclassics" as distinguished, no doubt, from "total" classic, and we shall not go into the subject of "serious" music and its antithesis, "frivolous" music.

Happily the critical terminology, if not necessarily the attitude it reveals, has gone pretty much into discard over the past few years. Consider Scott Joplin and, before him, Louis Moreau Gottschalk. While their zealous champions may have saddled these gifted musicians with heavier burdens than their talents might sustain, their belated discovery is an enrichment of the American musical heritage. Their popularity stimulates a reassessment not only of their work, but also that of others of humble or popular origin.

A musical work, of whatever dimension or intent, need not "sound" American to belong to our musical Americana category; the American musical scene without the European operetta accents of Victor Herbert, or the "absolute music" of Roger Sessions, or the experimentalism of George Crumb would be unthinkable. It is a wide-ranging music and, to borrow a phrase from Whitman, "contains multitudes."

The authentic music of the American Indian has had little effect on the evolution of American music—and the use of its themes by trained musicians resulted generally in the dissolution of the original. The first homespun songs were either of a religious or patriotic persuasion and all our folk songs, like other aspects of our culture, were importations. The early settlers brought hymns, psalms, and anthems with them. With little time for a cultivation of anything but a rough-hewn art, the colonists blended the folk with the sacred and added variations as creativity or memory lapse dictated. Native-born, self-proclaimed, and not necessarily tutored musicians began creating the earliest American music.

Our first self-made composer, and certainly one of the first of our truly American composers, was the tanner turned musician, William Billings. Though frequently damned by early critics, the songs of Billings, sacred and patriotic, were popular. The apocryphal story of the hanging of the two cats from Billings's tannery sign may be the first recorded example of American music criticism. But Billings, despite such opprobrium, prevailed and left behind a sturdy body of song.

Writing, as he himself stated, not "confin'd to any Rules for Composition," Billings produced folklike compositions of earthy power and uncommon beauty, among them the canon, "When Jesus Wept," and the popular Revolutionary War song, "Chester." He was but one—although undoubtedly the most colorful—among many native-born American composers who flourished toward the middle and end of the eighteenth century, most of whom practiced music as an avocation: Justin Morgan, the horse breeder; Andrew Law, the minister; Daniel Reed, the merchant; and the wonderfully named Supply Belcher, the tavern keeper. These men were members in good standing of what musicologists now generally refer to as our "First New England School."

These early composers shared with Billings the gift for homespun music—pungent, irregularly shaped, and robust, of plain, utilitarian beauty. Their popularity waned with the introduction of musical "standards," but the songs were preserved, folklike, by tradition in the South and the West.

Post-Revolutionary immigration and the rise of the cities along the Eastern Seaboard closed the "Yankee tunesmith" chapter of American music. The cities afforded the setting for the professional (European) trained musician and the music "industry." Public recitals and concerts were a natural consequence, as was the flourishing of the theater. Enter, thereupon, the cat-hangers with quills sharpened.

The homespun was rejected in favor of more skillfully fashioned imports. This was not a disaster, although it did detour some fascinating music into near limbo. It also introduced the concept of professionalism into music teaching, performance, and creativity. The music brought by the immigrant musicians, particularly that of Handel and Haydn, and of course their own compositions based on these models, could only have had a salutary influence on the American musician.

With Charleston, Philadelphia, New York, and Boston as the main hubs, music as a performing art, as public entertainment, radiated to other urban centers. However Europeanized it may have been, this diffusion established the roots for what would evolve into American "serious" music, the musical theater and, in time, even Tin Pan Alley. The marriage of art and business was consummated. Music came out of the kitchen and the choir loft into the recital hall and the bookkeeper's domain.

An important and popular early form of entertainment was the ballad opera that had been around, even in the colonies, before the Revolutionary War. *Flora, or Hob in the Well,* a one-act medley of songs, was presented in Charleston in 1735; fifteen years later, the granddaddy of all musical comedy, *The Beggar's Opera* (1728), was presented in New York. These and others of the period were of English origin. The first home-grown product, the work of one Andrew Barton (the composer's, or compiler's, name is unknown), was entitled *The Disappointment, or The Force of Credulity.* Its fate was a portent to future aspiring producers, composers, librettists, and lyricists—for it closed before opening night sometime in 1767.

It would be stretching a bit to attempt to date the birth of the American musical from these entertainments, but they are antecedents. Others could be mentioned: *Tammany: or, The Indian Chief,* with music by the English-born James Hewitt; with a book by Mrs. Anne Julia Hatton, the "opera" was as much political as a celebration of the Noble Red Man. A surviving fragment, "Alknomook (The Death Song of the Cherokee Indians)," is hardly captivating, although the work as a whole might be of historic significance: it may be the first Indian-inspired musical in which the original music was destroyed by a trained but unwittingly ethnocentric musician. Hewitt was, however, a substantial force in the early development of American music both in New York and Boston; he contributed to their cultural life with his own compositions, his music publishing business, and a number of musically gifted sons and daughters.

A contemporary of Hewitt's, Benjamin Carr, has been credited by some scholars with the first "musical," *The Archers: or, The Mountaineers of Switzerland*, its book based on the story of William Tell. Like Hewitt, Carr was English born and was successful as a publisher of music as well as of his weekly *Musical Journal*, which served to preserve the song, "Why, Huntress, Why?" from *The Archers* (1796). There is a great gap in time between the production of Carr's "opera" and the other favorite "first" American musical, *The Black Crook* (1866).

In form, unquestionably, *The Black Crook* was more closely related to the musical comedies that burgeoned during the 1920s, when the American musical truly came of age. The *Crook* was a mélange of song, ballet, girls, and extravagant theatrical effects. But it was the girls that created the most furor and no doubt helped to keep the show running for nearly 500 performances.

The Black Crook was initiated as a deep melodrama into which the girls were introduced literally by accident. The Academy of Music, New York, that was to have served as the showplace for a newly arrived French ballet, chanced to burn to the ground shortly before the scheduled opening. Thus unhoused, the girls were worked into *The Black Crook* (no doubt through the conniving of the producers) then in rehearsal at Niblo's Garden on Broadway and Prince Street. The author, Charles M. Barras, fought this incursion, fearing that their pulchritude would obscure his art. This art, it might be mentioned, was a hackish appropriation from several sources, ranging from *Faust* to *Der Freischuetz*. It was, however, obvious to all (if not author Barras) that even in its rehearsal stage *The Black Crook* was a sure-fire flop.

Art quickly succumbed to fiscal reality (a characteristic of the Broadway scene ever since) and Barras recanted with a cry of the nineteenth-century equivalent to "Bring on the girls!" and the show was on. All the ingredients were poured into the pot and boiled, resulting in an evening that began at 7:45 and ended at 1:15. *The Black Crook* was a smash hit, with its extravagant sets, complex scenic effects, hurricanes, deals with devils, flying angels, and, of course, the girls. *The Black Crook* was one big mishmash.

The "daring" costumes of the ballerinas incited denunciation from the clergy and the press. The most damning editorializing, published in the New York *Tribune*, was generally attributed to the neglect by the show's management to advertise in that paper. The editorials stimulated business more than the drama-page advertisement, and people—including respectable ladies, who attended demurely veiled—flocked to witness this early leg show, and to marvel at all the fancy stagecraft. Whatever its precise historical standing, *The Black Crook* was certainly one of the earliest of Broadway musicals.

But what sounds were heard between *The Archers*'s "Why, Huntress, Why?" and the *Crook*'s "You Naughty, Naughty Men"? Opera, concerts, and recitals multiplied, and music publishing expanded, all to the sweet song of the ringing cash register. The emigré "professors" had sparked the American taste for "cultivated" music: parlor songs and various forms of instrumental works from the chamber music of contemporary European masters to fanciful, very descriptive, piano pieces about battles, storms at sea, and other disasters. About two-thirds through this span, a form of entertainment that would become known as the minstrel show appeared. Even before the debut of the Virginia Minstrels at the Bowery Amphitheatre in New York (1843), the white man's caricature of the black had its precursors. It even had a rival, the Christy Minstrels, which claimed priority by one year. No matter; historically its time had come, despite the decided paucity of redeeming social values.

Blackface entertainers had been on the scene at least two decades before, however. Among the more notable were George Washington Dixon and Thomas Dartmouth Rice, who contributed not only a song but also a concept in "Jim Crow." "Daddy" Rice's act was an imitation of a true-life personality, complete with tattered costume, dialect, and an eccentric dance—unlike the stereotyping that would mark the minstrel show. Daniel D. Emmett, another pioneer and one of the Virginia Minstrels and later of Bryant's Minstrels, composed the memorable "Dixie's Land." Few, if any, of the minstrel's "Ethiopian songs" were the real thing—many were borrowed from various sources, including Italian and British pieces (for instance, "Zip Coon," better known as "Turkey in the Straw"). Authenticity was not the point, though many of the earlier minstrel, or plantation, songs were based on slave songs. As the form of the show evolved with a surge of popularity toward the end of the century, the true Negro contribution was lost in a welter of show-business stereotyping; but what was developing, once the burned cork was washed away, was vaudeville's burlesque and the revue.

During the waning period of the minstrel show only one black entertainer emerged—in blackface!—to contribute songs that belong among the classics of the earlier days. He was James Bland, who created such songs as "Carry Me Back to Old Virginny," "Oh, Dem Golden Slippers," and "In the Evening by the Moonlight," among others.

The most successful minstrel troupe was Christy's, which was active for at least a decade; more important, this group was to serve as an outlet for the "Ethiopian songs" of Stephen Foster.

Little needs to be said of Foster, our first great popular songwriter, except to point out that Ethiopian or "plantation melodies" made up but a small fraction of his output of more than 200 songs. A Pennsylvanian, Foster escaped the influence of the "professors" who dominated the music centers of the Eastern Seaboard. Born into a family with business inclinations, he was not encouraged in music. With meager musical training, and drawing upon the popular songs of his youth—the traveling minstrel shows that came to Pittsburgh and genuine plantation songs he heard on the wharves of the Ohio River—he published his first song, "Open Thy Lattice, Love," at the age of seventeen.

After a couple of successes, one of them being the popular "Oh! Susanna," Foster gave up his job as a bookkeeper to devote his energies to songwriting. His gift for melody was remarkable, his ear for the common, or vernacular, was unique. Much of his output could be classified as sentimental, but the direct simplicity of the best of the songs raises them above that category. Even the first of his Ethiopian songs to achieve phenomenal popularity, "Old Folks at Home," is touched with nostalgic longing—although by no means could it be described as blues.

This song's publication set the tone of Foster's future in songwriting: the first title page read: "Ethiopian Melody as sung by Christy's Minstrels. Written and Composed by E. P. Christy." Such false ascription was a fairly common practice (and may continue to this day); but the principal reason Foster acceded was to protect his already considerable reputation as a writer of "another style of music" (the genteel songs fit for parlor consumption). The great success of "Old Folks at Home" awakened Foster to his own potential, both financially and in terms of "public approbation," as he wrote to Christy, asking to have his own name restored to the sheet music of the song. Christy's reply, confined to the reverse of Foster's letter, was "vacillating skunk!" Although he received royalties from the song, Foster never did see his name on its sheet music in his lifetime.

Foster's initial desire for anonymity was justified by the attacks on the song in the press, among them *Dwight's Journal of Music*; the song's pervasiveness prompted a fellow composer, hymn-tunesmith Thomas Hastings, to fire off a communication to the *Musical Review and Choral Advocate* (May 1853) in which he anguished over little children's minds being exposed to such "poisonous trash," which was little more than "something from the lowest dregs of music and poetry."

Fortunately unperturbed, Foster continued to produce Ethiopian songs along with his ballads, duets, and modest instrumental pieces. For roughly a decade (1850-60), he created masterpieces in miniature, folklike and enduring (along with much uninspired hackwork). Although Foster could not be classified as a pioneer—he relied on conventional harmonies, and uncomplicated melodies and rhythmic figures—he was a true American original. He, instinctively perhaps, raised the so-called Ethiopian song above the minstrel-show level; the black voice heard in a Foster song belonged to a man of dignity and character, not the buffoon created by blackface comics. His contribution to our music, before an unhappy marriage and drink led to an early death at the age of thirty-seven, amounts to more than a dozen or two songs—most of them still sung around the world as American folk songs. He re-created the songs of the black man with rare understanding, and endowed popular song with unique artistry.

Although he composed various instrumental pieces, Foster did not aspire to the concert hall, the business of which flourished concurrently with the minstrel shows—although the twain rarely met. Still, by the mid- and late-nineteenth century, an aura of show business infected the concert field, what with the worship of imported virtuosos and a love of orchestral giantism—"Monster Concerts for the Masses."

An American-born contemporary of Foster's moved gracefully into that world and perhaps for the first time in American history crossed the cultural tracks between popular and serious music. He was, of course, the colorful Louis Moreau Gottschalk, born in New Orleans, but for a short flashing lifetime, citizen of the world.

Gottschalk was the first American musician to achieve worldwide recognition and acclaim. A child prodigy—his talent was revealed when Gottschalk was three—he was sent off to Paris to study at the age of thirteen and made an impressive debut shortly after his sixteenth birthday. Gottschalk's playing earned him the praise of Chopin and Berlioz. Not only were Gottschalk's pianistics admired; so were his original compositions, some of the most characteristic of which date to his teens in Paris. Some of these were based on Gottschalk's earliest musical memories from New Orleans—notably, the *bamboula*, a Louisiana Creole dance. It was this practice of drawing upon folk sources, national airs, and popular songs—an innovation Gottschalk introduced a half century before Dvorak so advised American composers—that should have earned him a position of eminence among American composers.

Gottschalk's virtuosity overshadowed his creativity; his original works, predominantly for piano, reveal the performer dominating the composer. A decided crowd-pleaser—an audience often jammed with swooning young ladies—Gottschalk gave them what they wanted, complete with keyboard histrionics. While it was reported he could play the works of others brilliantly, his programs were made up primarily of his own pieces in which he could display what must have been a phenomenal technique. He quickly became an international celebrity, the first American to impress Europeans who believed anyone born in the New World was either a savage or a mechanic.

Much of Gottschalk's output consists of romantic show-pieces and sentimental salon pieces, all skillfully wrought and eminently pianistic. His most compelling compositions were those based on Afro-American and Caribbean themes: *Bamboula; Banjo,* Op. 15; *El Cocoye; Souvenir de Porto Rico;* and *Creole Eyes.* Even his less exotic Americana have charm, among them *The Union,* his arrangement of George F. Root's "The Battle Cry of Freedom," *Columbia* (in which Foster's "My Old Kentucky Home" is quoted)—all of which anticipated similar handling of national airs by Charles Ives by at least a generation. But, for all his celebrity, Gottschalk inspired no school. His influence on his contemporaries was negligible; no younger composers took up his practice of adapting folk and popular themes in original compositions.

While the best of Gottschalk remains his smaller piano pieces, he did compose a number of orchestral works of merit, several of which have come to light only recently. While such pieces as *A Night in the Tropics* and the *Grande Tarantelle* are effectively entertaining in their original instrumentations, Gottschalk—a child of his time—dreamed of performing them, and often did, with orchestral and choral forces of literally hundreds. To the end, his flair for showmanship obscured his gift for musical invention. Dead at forty (of peritonitis, in 1869), Gottschalk could hardly be classed among the "great" composers, but he was a true original. He intimated an authentic American music and even jazz, long before anyone ever thought that such a phenomenon existed.

Not that there were no self-conscious Americanists, even before Gottschalk's brief time. Francis Hopkinson, a contemporary of Billings and James Lyon, claimed "the Credit of being the first Native of the United States who has produced a Musical Composition." Foreign-born Anton Philip Heinrich pursued American themes almost concurrently with Gottschalk, with much less skill and inventiveness. Though called "the Beethoven of America," he was in fact an amateur who began composing at around the age of forty, turning out such patriotic effusions as: *Dawning of Music in Kentucky; The Columbiad,* a "Grand American national chivalrous symphony"; *The Wildwood Troubadour,* in four movements, which essayed the "Genius of Harmony slumbering in the forest shades of America"; a number of pieces devoted to the Indian; and an inevitable waltz based on "Yankee Doodle." Around the same time two somewhat less eccentric Americans emerged as champions of the native-born composer, William Henry Fry and George F. Bristow. Fry was both a composer (*Leonora*, perhaps the first American opera) and a critic; in the latter role he raised his voice (he was also a lecturer) to protest the neglect of the work of American composers during the period when all that was recognized as worthwhile in music was a German import. Bristow, a violinist with the New York Philharmonic Society, joined Fry in the attack on the philharmonic for its neglect (biting the hand that fed) by labeling it "anti-American." In a dramatic gesture, Bristow resigned from the philharmonic. He returned soon after, and enjoyed playing in performances of several of his works—which for all Bristow's musical nationalism (he composed an opera based on Rip Van Winkle), though well wrought, lack the sparkle and snap of Gottschalk's work. This was a characteristic in common with most of the American compositions under the German influence.

The "best" of American-made music of this time was represented by the work of Lowell Mason, a New Englander who, as a composer of hymns, would certainly have rejected the work of a rough-and-ready Billings as not being "scientific" or lacking "correctness." Lowell Mason contributed to the Germanizing of American music in both his compositions and as an influential musical educator. It was in this field that his contribution was most important; his work was continued by various disciples and two sons, William and Daniel Gregory Mason.

Post-Civil War music in the United States and into the bathetic "Gay" Nineties consisted of several streams, some of them barely touching; Mason's educational theories were setting a base, however bland and unadventurous. Composers, many educated in Germany, produced imitations of their mentors in orchestral pieces and works for voice. Popular music was an eclectic blend, borrowing as the spirit moved from the more elevated forms: sentimental and lively songs, waltzes, reels, plantation melodies, marches (the staple of the traditional concert in the park), and other popular songs and dances.

One year before the death of the arch-American, Bristow, (in 1898, the year George Gershwin was born), a white bandmaster named William Krell published a piece entitled "Mississippi Rag." Krell was not the first ragtime composer, merely the first to get into print. Two years later, in 1899, an unknown black pianist-composer published his *Original Rags* and "Maple Leaf Rag"; he was, of course, Scott Joplin.

Essentially a piano music, ragtime can be traced back to authentic plantation songs, minstrel shows (with their banjo virtuosos), as well as the popular dances and marches that served to make the latter 1890s truly gay. Its conception was Negro: the idea of an accented melodic line over a steady bass— syncopation throughout, instead of an occasional offbeat. The practice began with Negro bands that played the lively jigs, earning them the sobriquet, "jig band." Applying the same technique to waltzes, schottisches, and marches brought on the cakewalk craze. Before the piano style was named *ragtime*, it was called "jig piano," an innocuous term until absorbed into the vocabulary of bigotry.

Joplin was not the only ragtime composer, but he was unquestionably the most gifted. A child prodigy and son of a slave, he was given, because of his obvious talent for music, a good, early musical education. Although he may well have had the technical equipment, it is unlikely that he could have made a name on the recital stage. (An early black pianist was Thomas Greene Bethune, known professionally as "Blind Tom." Although he was recognized as a fine pianist, he was exhibited during the 1860s as a freakish performer who, despite his blindness, could carry off amazing feats of memory and counterpoint: one tune in the left hand, another in the right, and simultaneously singing still another.)

Joplin proceeded along the standard path then open to a Negro musician: he began playing in saloons and brothels. Since ragtime (like jazz that came later) was primarily a way of playing, it took a musician of Joplin's abilities to be able to capture it on paper with any accuracy. There is, however, no glib explanation for his gift of melody and exquisite sense of form. With the publication of "Maple Leaf Rag," Joplin initiated the ragtime craze that spread through the music centers of the United States and even to Europe. Although not done to death by overexposure (television and radio then nonexistent, the phonograph in its infancy), ragtime spread via itinerant musicians, vaudeville, the last of the minstrel shows, sheet music, and piano rolls.

The vogue lasted roughly through Joplin's truncated lifetime (he died in 1917) and, despite the romanticized claims of his neglect, he was successful. His success inspired disciples, emulators, and exploiters. Among his worthy disciples were James Scott and Joseph Lamb (who was white), with perhaps secondary status going to Artie Matthews and Percy Wenrich. They were joined by amateurs across the land—there being a piano or a pianola in practically every American parlor at the turn of the century—to drum ragtime out of service. It was Tin Pan Alley, whose occupants recognized a source of profit as soon as a sample was presented, that killed the popularity with "plugging" and corruption of the style. (In the interest of historical accuracy it might be noted that Irving Berlin's "Alexander's Ragtime Band," published in 1911, is not and never was intended to be a rag; in Berlin's succinct definition, "it's a song about ragtime.")

The classic rag, as opposed to its Tin Pan Alley perversion, is gently lyrical, often unhurried, and not confined to the thirty-two-bar form. The hack form was often a showpiece and, as true ragtime waned, became flashier, faster, and emptier. The grace and beauty of Joplin's contribution was vanquished by mere showmanship. After the ragtime era diminished to a whisper, the popular image that remained was of a derby-hatted, untutored pianist, cigar in mouth, and sporting sleeve garters, pounding away at some trite tune. The vogue had worn and waned and by the time the United States embraced the "ideals" of what would come to be called the First World War (marching off to the jaunty strains of "Over There"), the newer, rougher sounds of jazz assailed the ear.

As before, it was a black invention adapted and exploited by the white-dominated music business. The advent of jazz, at least on a commercial basis, coincided with a certain coming of age in the musical theater. The minstrel shows, vaudeville, burlesque, plus the more genteel operettas imported from Austria, France, and England had added something to the form that was generally called *musical comedy*. The more American accents were contributed by such as Harrigan and Hart, Weber and Fields—right out of burlesque—and the arch-Americanist, George M. Cohan. Tin Pan Alley, by the end of the war, was a thriving business, ready to supply "what the public wanted."

The average product that sustained this unlikely locale (or state of mind) was songs based on the popular hits of the previous year. Thus what tinkled out of the alley could be traced back to the sentimental ballads, ethnic songs affronting various nationalities and races, ragtime distortions, and numerous maddening novelty numbers. Tin Pan Alley was not noted for literacy and musical excellence circa 1920.

But there were currents: real musicians were writing songs for musicals, among them the Irish-born Victor Herbert, the major link between the American musical theater and European operetta. His American successor was Jerome Kern, who, because of the work he did there, brought to America a touch of the English music hall and comic opera. In this same prewar setting for the flowering of the American lyric theater, a Russian-born American, Irving Berlin, with a natural, untutored gift for song, had also come upon the scene. If ever there was a twentieth-century American folk singer, the musical descendant of Billings and Foster, it would have to be Berlin. These three, Herbert, Kern, and Berlin, were the major influences of tremendous changes in American popular music in the twenties.

Associated with jazz was another sound that had begun to make itself heard—the blues. Like jazz, the blues had been around a long time in the black ghettos, but it was not until the form was defined on paper by a great black musician, W. C. Handy, that its appealing colorations spread throughout the world. (It is the tragedy of Charles Ives, whose use of popular and folk themes in his compositions made him a musical original, that he chose to create in a vacuum. He was, thus, not an "influence" during this formative period when American composers had turned their backs on Germany and went to France instead; Ives might have made quite an impact had he been more widely known before the 1920s.)

With all the ferment bubbling in the world of popular music, the musical theater, and jazz, all that was needed to bring it to a head was a catalyst, and it was there—money.

Postwar United States, seemingly with energy and money to burn, flourished economically and culturally for a decade that would be called, among other things, the *Jazz Age*. It was an urban phenomenon primarily, with the major center New York, home of Broadway, Tin Pan Alley, Carnegie Hall, Greenwich Village, the Metropolitan Opera, and Wall Street. The news, trends, feuds, personalities, aesthetic currents, and styles from the art centers of the world (notably, then, Paris and Vienna) converged on New York for dissemination to the rest of the country. Some Americans, believing their native land had become crass, sought refuge in the more cultural setting of Paris. The exiles wrote about home; those artists who remained home longed for Paris. Both created a vital American art.

The "serious" composers, most of them unaware of Charles Ives and determined to make a break with the nineteenth-century Germanic yoke, sought out Nadia Boulanger in Paris. The more "radical" composers turned a fascinated ear toward Schoenberg's Vienna. But most stayed home, especially the popular and theater composers. They had to make do with what they had.

Many of the new songwriters were first-generation Americans whose parents had emigrated from Russia to escape the pogroms. The major exceptions were Irving Berlin, who was brought to the United States as a very young child, and Cole Porter, whose Midwestern roots were deep. Porter had money and spent much of the twenties in Europe in splendid exile.

Most of the other songwriters had in common a Jewish—though not very Orthodox—New York background, a great interest in the theater, a striving for excellence, and a zeal to be assimilated, to be American in the best nonchauvinistic sense. They had good literary or musical educations. Columbia University produced Oscar Hammerstein II, Lorenz Hart, and Richard Rodgers; the City College—Ira Gershwin, E. Y. Harburg, and Irving Caesar.

By the mid-twenties it became clear that a new quality had come to the art of popular song, especially as it was employed in the lyric theater. The words to the songs were literate, witty, polished, and pointed enough to qualify as good light verse. The music, too, was well crafted, frequently surprisingly sophisticated in melodic invention and rhythmic snap; the songs were harmonically rich, unlike the standard one-finger Tin Pan Alley products. The one concession—and that would also be abandoned as the spirit moved the writer—was to the standard thirty-two-bar song form. Within this constricted pattern the new generation created an unequaled collection of song and dance.

In the best of the work—George and Ira Gershwin, Rodgers and Hart, Porter, Berlin—words ("lyrics") and music melded into a single unit, although Kern and Vincent Youmans were not always well served by their lyricists. The music and words were closely related to native speech; to the rhythms, curves, and sense of the language.

George Gershwin, a true musical "go-getter," went one step further in bringing this musical vernacular into the concert hall. At the time—1924, the year of the *Rhapsody in Blue*—it was mislabeled jazz, though it was really a blend of Tin Pan Alley, Broadway bits of classical music, and some elements of jazz, but it was all Gershwin. No innovator, Gershwin simply drew upon those materials he knew from his study of the piano, harmony, and counterpoint as a youngster, his stint in Tin Pan Alley as a "piano pounder," and his belief that there could be quality, not just quantity, in American popular music. He left the unique orchestration of the *Rhapsody* to Ferde Grofé, since the latter was familiar with the makeup of the Paul Whiteman orchestra—and since Gershwin, busy with a new show score, had but two or three weeks in which to turn out a work for Whiteman's so-called Experiment in Modern Music. Grofé later prepared a full score of the *Rhapsody in Blue*; all other Gershwin orchestral works and his opera, *Porgy and Bess*, were orchestrated by the composer.

The impact of the *Rhapsody in Blue* was immediate and widespread: It established Gershwin as a fresh new voice in American music; it ushered in a genre frequently termed *symphonic jazz* (a contradiction in terms) and a host of imitators; it earned Gershwin his first serious accolades and diatribes, rendering him controversial and therefore commercially exploitable. The commission for his next work, which would be the *Concerto in F*, came from the New York Symphony Society; this was followed by another, resulting in *An American in Paris*. Not the least of Gershwin's contributions, whatever one thinks of his works, is that he dramatized, glamorized, and humanized the American composer.

Whiteman reigned as the "King of Jazz" (few at the time had heard of Louis Armstrong), and for a time seriously pursued a career on the concert stage, hoping, but vainly, to turn up another *Rhapsody in Blue*. He commissioned new works from his own Ferde Grofé, among them *Mississippi Suite* and the *Grand Canyon Suite*; and from Deems Taylor (*Circus Day*); John Alden Carpenter (*A Little Bit of Jazz*); and Dana Suesse (*Blue Moonlight, Symphonic Waltzes,* and *Jazz Concerto*). Most of these

pieces reveal a period charm, as Whiteman shifted from concert
hall to dance hall. He continued to encourage such Americana,
a great number of which repeated the pattern of the *Rhapsody
in Blue*, complete with busy opening and a richly melodic
middle section. These were often lifted from the greater work,
lyricized, and converted into popular songs. Out of *Deep Purple*
(Peter De Rose) came the song of the same name and "Lilacs in
the Rain," and from *Park Avenue Fantasy* (Matty Malneck and
Frank Signorelli) came "Stairway to the Stars." By the thirties,
Whiteman had been dethroned by such real jazzmen as Armstrong, Ellington, et al. Still Whiteman had made a contribution,
not only with his commissioning of the *Rhapsody in Blue* but also
by the encouragement of popular composers on leave from Tin
Pan Alley and by nurturing jazz musicians in his ample orchestra.
Whiteman was among the first to lead what would eventually
be called a big band, characterized by skilled musicians and
very musicianly arrangements and orchestrations of popular
songs of the time.

The more experimental musical activity during the twenties was produced by Henry Cowell, a friend of Ives, and his
friends: Carl Ruggles, Wallingford Riegger, and John J. Becker.
Aaron Copland, fresh from Boulanger's classes and eager
"to find a new music that would speak of universal things in
a vernacular of American speech rhythms," applied a French-
Stravinskyan polish to jazz (*Music for the Theatre, Piano
Concerto*) before finding his own voice in the hard-edged masterpiece, *Piano Variations*. Copland, like Gershwin, did not believe
an enduring musical movement could be based on what they
called jazz, although both absorbed and used certain jazz characteristics in rhythm and harmony. Copland, initially, deliberately
avoided the quotation of folk materials, but found them attractive
and useful when composing his popular, very American, ballets,
such as *Appalachian Spring* (another masterpiece), *Rodeo*, and
Billy the Kid.

The more experimental musical activity during the twenties was produced by Henry Cowell, a friend of Ives, and his
friends: Carl Ruggles, Wallingford Riegger, and John J. Becker.
The more conservative school was headed by Howard Hanson
(important, like Copland, as an influential teacher), Walter Piston,
John Alden Carpenter, and John Powell. Some consciously employed American themes; others avoided them, preferring to
compose an abstract music free of all national association.
Chief among these was Roger Sessions. Active at this same
time were such a varied group as Roy Harris, Randall Thompson,

Douglas Moore, and Virgil Thomson, all of whom would manipulate American themes and, through their example and teach-
ings, influence all that followed in American music.

It was during the twenties, too, that the recognized
emergence of the Negro as a composer of concert music occurred;
the vogue of "jazz" contributed its quota of promotional interest.
This did nothing for Francis Johnson (1792-1844), but it did
create a wider (that is, white) market for the blues of W. C.
Handy, whose works, some original and others based on traditional melodies, were played by various "schools" of jazz performers formed across the land (all hoping, however, to come
to New York) in New Orleans, Kansas City, Chicago, and New
York itself. Each school had its own sound based on instrumentation and its members' capabilities.

Among the first of the black composers to make the transition from popular to concert hall was William Grant Still (who
arranged for Paul Whiteman and, later, Artie Shaw). His *Afro-
American Symphony*, which dates from 1930, has been performed
widely and regularly and is but one in a large, valuable body
of works, rooted in the black experience if not necessarily on
ethnic musical materials. Other American Negro composers who
have made substantial contributions to our concert music have
been R. Nathaniel Dett (best known for his *Juba Dance*) and the
younger Howard Swanson, who has written extraordinary songs
as well as orchestra pieces, including a prize-winning *Short
Symphony* (1950). In the generation following Still's, a wide
spectrum of musical expression has evolved in the works of
such composers as Ulysses Kay, Arthur Cunningham, George
Walker, and Stephen Chambers. The sound ranges from the
blues inspired to the most abstract chromaticism.

"American music is not jazz," observed the late, honored
critic Paul Rosenfeld, who immediately proceeded to hoist
himself with: "Jazz is not music." Even the perceptive, astute, and
sensitive could go astray (though his first statement is valid).
In much the same brusque, categorical manner, popular song
currents also were dismissed. That the two were often confused,
especially by "serious" critics, is another tale. History has a
disconcerting, inexorable way of being hard on people who would
make Large and Definitive Statements.

George Gershwin, not a Rosenfeld favorite, had another
view: "Jazz I regard as an American folk-music; not the only

one, but a very powerful one which is probably in the blood
and feeling of the American people more than any other style
of folk-music." He believed, in 1933, that there was no single
American folk music, "but many different folk-musics. . . Jazz,
ragtime, Negro spirituals and blues, Southern mountain songs,
country fiddling, and cowboy songs," all of which could be used
"in the creation of American art-music. . . ." At the same time
Gershwin recognized the validity of nonfolk-based music by
composers who had "developed highly individual styles and
methods."

Gershwin continued producing songs as well as concert
works, fusing the two in *Porgy and Bess* in 1935, just two years
before his early death. The Depression 1930s brought a change
to the Broadway scene and with it a new generation. Harold
Arlen, Arthur Schwartz, Howard Dietz, Burton Lane, and Kay
Swift brought a new artistry to popular songwriting. But with
the dwindling away of the Broadway scene (although important
revues, often with political bite, and musicals continued to be
done), many of the finest songwriters went to Hollywood. The
result was a flowering of the musical film, particularly in
motion pictures starring Fred Astaire and Ginger Rogers (with
songs by Vincent Youmans, Jerome Kern and Dorothy Fields,
the Gershwins, Cole Porter, and Irving Berlin). The art—or
science—of film background music also came into its own,
although most sounded like warmed-over clichés of the Romantics
in this special field initially dominated by European-born and
-trained musicians. Except for a brief, songlike theme, most
film background music was designed to be unobtrusive; the
theme, perhaps fitted with words, would serve to "plug the
picture." Often, without the visuals, these scores seemed undeveloped and repetitious. But even if developed, the sound was
modernized Tchaikovsky.

In time, however, scores were created for films by Virgil
Thomson, Bernard Herrmann, Aaron Copland, Jerome Moross,
Alex North, and, later, Leonard Bernstein that functioned
effectively in their films and also as concert works. In truth,
work of the caliber produced by this handful of composers is
the exception. They have drawn not only on their skills but
also on a vocabulary based on their musical experiences, and
then applied it to the most accessible of the popular arts. As
well-rounded composers, they generally could escape the atten-

tions of studio orchestrators and arrangers. Not that Hollywood orchestrators and arrangers are necessarily depredators, but they tend too often to depend on the lush cliché rather than imagination. Still such composer-arrangers as Robert Russell Bennett, who worked in Hollywood during the Astaire-Rogers period, enhanced the work of others; likewise the miniaturist, Alec Wilder, who did a wonderful job on composer Hugh Martin's music for the documentary on Grandma Moses, *New England Suite*. Bennett returned to Broadway in time to participate in the musical renaissance that began in the early forties with Rodgers and Hart's *Pal Joey* and the musical *Lady in the Dark* by Kurt Weill, orchestrated by Ira Gershwin.

The renaissance blossomed with the several Rodgers and Hammerstein plays with music, and with such characteristic American operas (the term *musical comedy* hardly serves) as *Bloomer Girl* (Harold Arlen/E. Y. Harburg), *On the Town* (Leonard Bernstein/Betty Comden-Adolph Green), *Annie Get Your Gun* (Irving Berlin), *Finian's Rainbow* (Burton Lane/E. Y. Harburg), *Kiss Me Kate* (Cole Porter), and *Guys and Dolls* (Frank Loesser). These and others of high quality were characterized by memorable songs, often directly related to the plot; extended instrumental passages, the work mostly of the arranger, were composed for ballet sequences, a practice that reached a peak in Bernstein's *West Side Story*. The impetus carried into the fifties in the works of Richard Adler and Jerry Ross (*The Pajama Game, Damn Yankees*), Frederick Loewe and Alan Jay Lerner (*My Fair Lady, Camelot*) until swamped by the youth movement and its quota of rock musicals, still too close to us for evaluation. Of the younger generation, Stephen Sondheim has proved consistent and inventive, working within the traditions that began in the twenties and yet contributing something new: for example, his lyrics to the music of Jule Styne in *Gypsy* and in his words and music (and not forgetting the orchestrations of Jonathan Tunick) in such musicals as *Follies* and *A Little Night Music*.

American ballet, aside from its function in musicals, began its rise during the Second World War, which served to promote Americana. Aaron Copland's popular pieces come immediately to mind, since both theme of the dance and of the music are American. John Alden Carpenter's *Crazy Kat* and *Skyscrapers* date back to the twenties. Virgil Thomson produced his *Filling Station* in 1938, and evoked wonderfully the popular songs of the time; Jerome Moross constructed pungently witty variations on the quasi-folk song *Frankie and Johnny*; Leonard Bernstein's brash, youthful *Fancy Free*, with its racy dances and jazzy rhythms, is a charming memento of the bittersweet war years. Morton Gould demonstrated his mastery of American forms in *Interplay*, which draws on numerous sound sources: the blues, the eight-to-the-bar boogie-woogie bass, pop song, the sound of the thirties' big band. A more serious theme may be found in Gould's *Lizzie Borden* or in William Schuman's *Undertow*. Hershey Kay created successful ballet scores based on the works of Gottschalk (*Cakewalk*) and John Philip Sousa (*Stars and Stripes*), reminders of the efficacy of smaller forms.

In this special vein—unpretentious shorter pieces patently related to popular music, but fashioned and developed with unique skill—we have the works of such composers as arranger/orchestrators Alec Wilder and Leroy Anderson. The former fashions exquisite cameos, haunting songs, and occasional pieces with a deft touch: a musician's musician. Anderson, urbane, witty, Harvard graduate, was fortunate in having the Boston Pops Orchestra at hand practically the moment the ink had dried on a manuscript. The popularity of his early (1938) *Jazz Pizzicato* and its sequel, *Jazz Legato*, led to the association with Arthur Fiedler and the Pops—and subsequently to such extraordinarily popular (and musically satisfying) instrumentals as *The Syncopated Clock*, *Serenata*, and *Blue Tango*. Yankee born, like Billings and Ives, Anderson was content to arrange and orchestrate (mainly for the Pops) and to create his musical vignettes (out of a remarkable musical erudition), remarking with a shrewd Yankee twinkle in his eye, "light music is a serious business."

The time span from Billings, whose voice cried in the wilderness, to Anderson's jukebox and recording proliferation is not an especially long one. But during that time a true American music evolved, both "serious" and "popular," interacting to sing with an American accent, with the wall that ostensibly stood between the two characteristics not amounting to a hill of beans. What will remain another 200 years from now is academic; we are too often preoccupied with immortality that none will ever see. Some structures created by man—buildings, novels, symphonies, songs—are beautifully proportioned and unconsciously designed to endure. That they may is, ultimately, immaterial to the architect, author, composer, or songwriter. But to future generations: This heritage will be the present.

3

Social and Moral Music: The Hymn

Austin B. Caswell

In thinking about this subject, I asked my colleague next door (who has a phenomenal bibliographic memory) if he had heard anything new on American hymnody. Without batting an eye he answered, "American hymnody? I don't know anything at all about that." Though my colleague specialized in Haydn, he has a wide contact with other areas of music, many of them far removed from Haydn, Vienna, and the eighteenth century. Yet he drew the line at American hymnody and put it into the category of less important areas of music. Why?

I think there are a number of reasons why scholars tend to ignore this aspect of musical history, some reasons connected with the fact that to this day American listeners still turn to Europe for their repertoire, their criteria of taste, and their performers. This cultural inferiority complex is reflected in (and to some extent caused by) certain developments in American hymnody. Another reason has to do with the fact that few educated persons in the Western world today consider organized religion to be either personally or culturally important. The church is simply no longer one of society's movers and shakers; and when our condescending attitude on this score is combined with our bemused tolerance of our Puritan ancestors' primitive state with regard to morality, intellectual and political freedom, and aesthetic elevation, it is little wonder that we prefer to think of America's early religious culture (and its music) as quaint or historically interesting, but not a valid form of artistic expression, nor one that can speak to us today.

American hymnody, directly descended from that of the eighteenth century, is very much alive today and can be heard in both black and white fundamentalist churches across the country. But with the exception of a few researchers, performers, and composers, we have chosen to consider this heritage as a phenomenon connected with certain groups (usually the ones we associate with a lack of the proper cultural badges), but certainly not a part of the heritage of us *all*, for *all* of us to be proud of. A few composers of the past generation (such as Charles Ives, Aaron Copland, and Virgil Thomson) made use of this hymnody in their compositions, but it did not stick. A few concert performers, notably black singers (the late Paul Robeson, Leontyne Price), have included American hymnody in their repertoire, but this, too, is the exception. Why is it that we are uncomfortable with our heritage of hymnody, unlike the composers of France, Germany, England, and Italy, who have made use of Catholic chant and Protestant hymns as far back as history can go?

Most of the hymns currently in use in the predominant sects of American Protestantism are from a nineteenth-century movement that Gilbert Chase calls the *genteel tradition* and H. Wiley Hitchcock the *cultivated tradition*. These labels refer to the effort of the prospering urban, American middle class to acquire culture, develop "scientific" and "progressive" attitudes, and in general become more like their image of the sophisticated European and less like their image of the bumpkins who populated the United States.

This movement put a serious and still observable blight on the growth of a healthy attitude of Americans toward their own musical culture, an attitude not limited to church music then or now, but one that has affected all our music and all our musical institutions—the composer, performer, and listener as well as the music curricula from elementary school through the university and its graduate division. Its basic tenet was that if a more scientific approach to a problem could be discerned, it was society's duty to adopt it and apply it, even in the face of other criteria. No other qualification was required. In music "cultured" and "sensitive" leaders discerned that the more scientific (and therefore "better") approach to composition was to be found among European composers, and that it was therefore the duty of the American musician to improve the cultural standards of his countryman by weaning him away from the unimproved crudities of his homegrown musical traditions, and instilling in him a taste for the advanced product of Europe. This would raise his cultural level and thus improve his lot on earth (and move him yet another step along the road toward the eventual perfection of man). The cultural inferiority complex that settled as fallout from these efforts is with us yet.

In church music this movement is best seen in the efforts of Lowell Mason (1792-1872), whose career dominates the cultivated musical aspirations of church and school during the first half of the nineteenth century. Mason was born in Massachusetts, and virtually all of his professional career was spent in Boston. He had professional training on organ, piano, flute, clarinet, and other instruments, and while working as a bank teller in Savannah, Georgia, received compositional training from a German immigrant musician, F. L. Abel. As a church organist and choirmaster in Savannah, he quite naturally spent some time compiling his own collection of favorite hymns and making new arrangements by setting hymn texts to tunes he admired. This collection contained a few of Mason's own tunes, but was dominated by arrangements of compositions by European composers: Beethoven, Haydn, Mozart, et al. In searching for a publisher, Mason and his anthology came in contact with the Boston Handel and Haydn Society (its very name communicating its continental orientation), which agreed to sponsor the publication of the anthology and to lend its name to the title. The title page of the first edition, which appeared in 1822, featured the names of several European composers. In this anthology Mason incorporated a signal technological advance, the figured "base" for accompaniment purposes. It is worth recalling that this scientific improvement had already disappeared from European musical practice by the time Mason adopted it in Boston. The orientation of the Handel and Haydn Society can be discerned by a few quotes from the preface to the first edition. They find themselves encouraged that "visible improvement has taken place in the style of singing, and consequently in the taste of the community. . .'' but while "much has been done, they are confident that all *scientific* and disinterested persons will agree with them that much still remains undone. . .[emphasis added].'' In addition to introducing arrangements from composers "whose mighty talents have been displayed and acknowledged throughout Europe. . .they have engaged themselves in reharmonizing the American psalm tunes they kept." This was deemed necessary because "the harmonies were mostly added by inferior composers. . ." and also since "the longest usage cannot reconcile science and correct taste with false harmony. It has been found indispensably necessary to introduce changes into the accompanying parts. . . .''[1]

The preface is followed by an extensive pedagogical "Introduction to the Art of Singing," which continued in the traditions of all American church anthologies. On the other hand, many "advanced" and "scientific" concepts were included, such as Rameau's designations of chord functions (tonic, dominant, subdominant, et al.), a discussion of the modulatory figures, and the use of figured bass.

Most of the hymns are in four parts, which marks a break with the past, but as is admitted in the preface, traditional taste dictated the retention of many older settings and the placement of tunes in the tenor part in the seventeenth-century manner. In this collection are many hymns that have become widely known and are in current use in American Protestantism today. One is "Duke Street," which is usually used with the text, "Jesus shall reign where'er the sun doth his successive journeys run," by Isaac Watts (1674-1748). The tune is by J. Hatton (died 1793). Another example well known today is "Italian Hymn," arranged by Mason from the music of Felice de Giardini (1716-96). Among other well-known arrangements Mason made are "Austrian Hymn" (from Haydn), now usually sung to the text, "Glorious things of Thee are spoken," by John Newton (1725-1807), and a setting called "Evening Hymn" in which Mason makes use of Thomas Tallis's famous four-part canon but "uncanonizes" it into a four-part setting and applies appoggiaturas to the point where the melody is all but hidden.

The success of this collection was the beginning of a profitable and influential career for Mason. The collection itself went into twenty-two editions, made him a wealthy man, and got him elected president of the Handel and Haydn Society in 1827. From this vantage point he could see that there was great "progress" to be made by working his reforms on the public-school systems. In 1832, he founded the Boston Academy of Music, which offered free musical training to Boston children, and by 1838 he had not only moved the Boston public-school system to include music as part of its curriculum but had been installed as superintendent of the new discipline as well. From this position he influenced the future course of American public-school music by pronouncing that "the chief value of music. . . will be social and moral" and that "music should be cultivated and taught. . .as a sure means of improving the affections and of ennobling, purifying, and elevating the whole man."[2]

Adding anthologies of public-school music to his production, Mason produced at least twenty-three separate collections of church and school music during his lifetime (not counting re-editions) and contributed 1,200 of his own compositions to the American repertoire. Among these are "From Greenland's Icy Mountains," "Nearer My God to Thee," and "My Faith Looks Up to Thee." A profound indication of how deeply Mason's hymns have become rooted in the American culture may be seen in the fact that when Charles Ives (a noted anti-European among other things) wanted to express an unshakable New England faith or traditions coming from generations of Puritan experience, he found the associations for which he was looking in the hymns of Lowell Mason, as evidenced in his *Symphony no. 4* where "From Greenland's Icy Mountains" is used as the basis for the fugue in the "Third Movement" and "Nearer My God to Thee" appears in the first.

H. W. Hitchcock has characterized Mason's musical style as one of "genteel correctness, neat and tidy in harmony and form, bland in rhythm and melodic thrust,"[3] while Chase accuses him of "thrusting the native American musical tradition. . .into the background, while opening the gates for a flood of colorless imitations of the 'European masters.' "[4]

Thus the influence of Lowell Mason had two important aspects: He taught American Protestants to know and love hymn-tunes that were not of American origin, and, more significant, he (along with the genteel tradition of which he was merely one part) taught Americans to look toward Europe for cultural guidance, and to be suspicious of the quality of any native

American product. The heritage of this influence is that until quite recently we have all but forgotten the American traditions of hymnody and psalmody that preceded the nineteenth century.

What do we know of the music of the seventeenth-century New England Puritans? The popular image is one of a stern, formidable asceticism that forbade all forms of artistic expression. This view of the Puritans as bluenoses who disapproved of music is completely erroneous. They did not condemn music or any other art. What they *did* do, however, was to hold music up to examination by the standard of morality and human behavior. If secular music led to immoral conduct, it was not to be permitted; but if it provided welcome enjoyment, if it lifted the heart and soothed the soul, then it was encouraged. Gilbert Chase has found voluminous evidence revealing that the New England Puritans owned and played instruments extensively, and enjoyed music as a social pleasure just as all Western cultures have. Religious music they not only permitted but viewed as a necessity as well. Like all Western religious sects, they recognized that congregational singing served a number of functions that could not be fulfilled as well (if at all) by any other activity, and it provided the emotional release necessary in a hard-working, strictly organized society. It also provided the opportunity for affirmation of congregational unity in communal worship, and its texts embodied the Puritan theology so that their memorization and constant use ensured the proper level of informed belief in each church member. One aspect of their "puritanical" outlook must be noted and not misinterpreted. They did limit religious music to voices alone; no instruments (not even the organ) were permitted. But this was not because they disapproved of instrumental music on moral grounds as is so often implied, but because instrumental music was too close to the musical practices of Roman Catholicism. Too often the exclusion of instrumental music from worship has been used as the prime example of the "puritanical" hatred of all art. It is simply not true.

Their singing was congregational. There was no use of the trained soloist singing to (or for) the congregation. The benefits of music were entirely participatory; there was no thought given to the worshipper as *hearer* of music, he was to be a *doer*. In their return to what they saw as the scriptural fundamentals of Christianity, the Puritans turned to the Psalms of David as the source of almost all their texts. These texts were of scriptural source and were originally intended to be sung; there could be no more authentic source. The psalm texts were set to unharmonized melodies that were for the most part stanzas of four symmetrical lines each, repeated again and again to accommodate all the verses of the psalm. But there was a problem in this process, one that led to some peculiar results in terms of poetry. The psalms in their original Hebrew are not rhymed, nor are they in most English translations of the Bible; they are best described as blank verse. Nor are they arranged in stanzas of four lines, although a large majority of them are in couplets. What the English Puritan movement did was to force this blank verse into rhymed stanzas, which made it easier to fit to a preexisting tune and perhaps easier to memorize, but it often had the effect of making a flowing lyric poetry chunky and stolid, if not actually clumsy. For example, let us take Psalm 23, which in the King James Bible reads

The Lord is my shepherd,
I shall not want.
He maketh me to lie down in green pastures,
He leadeth me beside the still waters,
He restoreth my soul.

The *Bay Psalm Book* reads

The Lord to me a shepherd is,
Want therefore shall not I,
He in the folds of tender grass
Doth cause me down to lie.

What can be seen in this short example is that the Puritans sacrificed flowing language and flights of metaphor for rhyme and straightforward statements of the fundamentals of faith. This rough-hewn sturdiness is one of the things that proves attractive in Puritan psalmody, for it matches the musical approach exactly.

But where did the Puritans get their music? Did they compose it for the occasion? Very seldom. In most cases they borrowed it. This process of taking a previously known melody and adapting it to different words may be deprecated by us as unoriginal, but it was an accepted approach to composition

5. PSALME 100 (L.M.)

1551

The Book of Psalmes
Henry Ainsworth
(*Amsterdam, 1612*)

Louis Bourgeois
(c. 1510–c. 1561)

SHowt to Je - ho - vah, al the earth. Serv . ye Je - ho - vah with glad - nes:

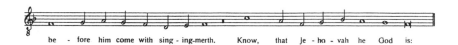

be - fore him come with sing - ing - merth. Know, that Je - ho - vah he God is:

2
Its he that made us, and not wee;
his folk, and sheep of his feeding.
O with confession enter yee
his gates, his courtyards with praising:

3
confess to him, bless ye his name.
Because Jehovah he good is:
his mercy ever is the same:
and his faith, unto al ages.

Henry Ainsworth
(c. 1570–1623)

5a. PSEAUME CXXXIV (L.M.)

1551

Trente quatre pseaumes
French-Genevan Psalter
(*Geneva, 1551*)

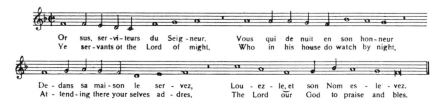

Or sus, ser - vi - teurs du Seig - neur, Vous qui de nuit en son hon - neur
Ye ser - vants ot the Lord of might, Who in his house do watch by night,

De - dans sa mai - son le ser - vez, Lou - ez - le, et son Nom es - le - vez.
At - tend - ing there your selves ad - dres, The Lord our God to praise and bles.

Théodore de Bèze
(1519–1605)

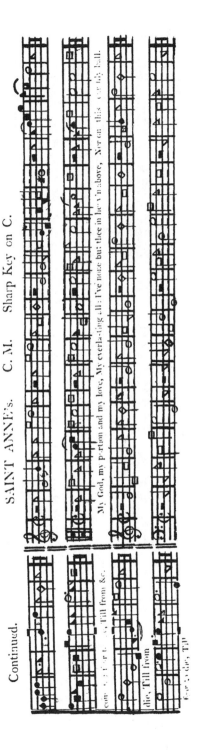

SAINT ANNE's.   C. M.   Sharp Key on C.

Continued.

My God, my portion and my love, My everlasting all: I've none but thee in heav'n above, Nor on this earthly ball.

com___ ___t er te____, Till from &c.

die, Till from

For___ die, Till

KEDRON. L. M.

Dare.

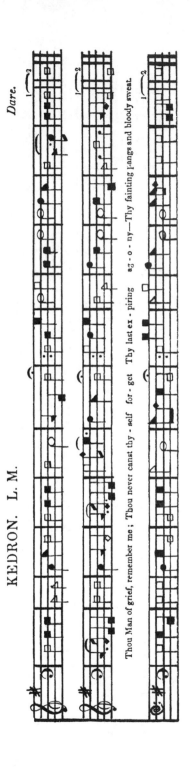

Thou Man of grief, remember me; Thou never canst thy-self for-get Thy last ex-piring ag - o - ny—Thy fainting pangs and bloody sweat.

URANIA,
or
A Choice Collection of Psalm-Tunes, Anthems, and Hymns,
From the most approv'd Authors, with some Entirely New;
in Two, Three, and Four Parts,
The whole Peculiarly Adapted to the Use of
CHURCHES, and PRIVATE FAMILIES:
To which are Prefix'd
The Plainest, & most Necessary Rules of Psalmody.
By JAMES LYON, A.B.

Hen Dawkins fecit 1761

Philada

until the nineteenth century. All composers felt free to borrow
and rearrange any melody they liked, including the great J. S.
Bach, whose list of borrowings is almost as long as Handel's.
In the field of sacred music the Puritans had a fine precedent
in the activity of Martin Luther, who in his enthusiasm for music
for his new sect borrowed from the Catholic Church, the tavern,
and the repertoire of love songs.

However, the Puritans used few of Luther's sources, and
made no use of the great body of chorale tunes produced by the
Lutheran movement. Instead they turned to the French Huguenot
movement and John Calvin (Jean Chauvin), whose influence was
so strong in all of English Protestantism. From Calvin they took
the idea of vocal psalmody as the only form of music acceptable
for worship, and also the idea of rhymed verses set to a single
melody and sung without instrumental accompaniment.

Calvin and his Huguenot followers had set up their center
of activity in Geneva in 1536, and very soon developed there a
center of theological activity attracting all types of Protestants
from all over Europe. Almost immediately Calvin directed that the
Book of Psalms be translated into French rhymed verses and set
to music, and by 1551 a Calvinist Psalter was published in
Geneva with translations and poetry by Clément Marot and
Théodore de Bèze and unharmonized tunes by Louis Bourgeois.
In 1562 English Protestants brought out a psalter of their own
(known as the *Sternhold-Hopkins Psalter*), which in its many
borrowings from the Geneva psalter shows that the English had
benefited from the French experiments. It used the same rhymed
verses and contained many of the same monophonic tunes used
by the Huguenots. If we trace the development of English
Protestant psalters, we can observe a continuous line of development away from the simple unharmonized tunes of the Sternhold-
Hopkins toward more "artful" settings of the time by professional composers whose main concerns lay with sophistication
of harmony and counterpoint, and the subtle treatment of the
meanings and emotions of the text.

But American developments did not derive from this movement toward musical sophistication. A group that we know as the
Pilgrims, but who were then known as the Separatists, rejected
this very sophistication and exiled themselves to Holland. There
they published their own psalter in 1612, which reverted to the
original Calvinist simplicity and made use of the old French

tunes. It was entitled *The Booke of Psalms, Englished in both Prose and Metre*, and was assembled by the Reverend Henry Ainsworth. It gives primary attention to the Psalm text and its rhymed version; the music consists of unharmonized tunes (only thirty-nine in all) of very limited range, melodic activity, and rhythm. One of the tunes Ainsworth borrowed from the Geneva psalter has lasted to the present day and is known by Americans of many different heritages as "Old Hundred" (Psalm 100) or, "Praise God from whom all blessings flow." A transcription of its appearance in the Ainsworth psalter, published on the same page with its French original from the Geneva psalter, shows both to have the abbreviation LM in parentheses immediately following the Psalm number. It refers to Long Meter—four lines of eight syllables each—which can be easily observed by counting the phrases and syllables in either the English or the French version of the tune. Other meters commonly in use in English and French psalters of the time were

Four lines of 6, 6, 8, and 6 syllables, known as
   Short Meter
Four lines of 8, 6, 8, and 6 syllables, known as
   Common Meter
Eight lines of 8, 6, 8, 6, 8, 6, 8, and 6 syllables,
   known as *Common Meter Double*

plus many irregular patterns that bear no name or abbreviation. By fitting their rhymed translations to one of these meters, many different psalms could be sung to the same tune, and conversely one psalm could be sung to a number of different tunes. The Ainsworth psalter contained fifteen different meters and thirty-nine different tunes, which afforded considerable variety in the singing of the 150 psalms. Unfortunately, later psalters printed in New England reduced the number of meters by half and tended to make use of only the regular and more symmetrical of them.

The first of these New England psalters was known as the *Bay Psalm Book* and its appearance in 1640 makes it the first book printed in New England. It was compiled by the Reverends Robert Mather, Thomas Wild, and John Elliott and was called *The Whole Booke of Psalms Faithfully translated into English metre*. It enjoyed twenty-seven editions by 1762, but contained no musical notation until the ninth edition of 1698, which printed thirteen tunes. It used only six meters, and the earlier editions advised the singers to use the tunes printed in previous English psalters (which indicated that the New England Puritans were familiar with such psalters even a generation or two after having left England). Its notation, as found in the 1698 edition, uses bar lines to mark the ends of phrases; instead of a text being printed under the notes, we see the letter f, s, l, or m under each note. These are abbreviations for *fa, sol, la,* and *mi,* and are obviously sight-reading aids for the congregational singer. But why only four syllables, why not *do, re,* and *ti*? There is an explanation (if not a reason) that we shall get to shortly. Another step has been taken: the tune is given an accompanying bass line to afford a harmonic framework.

After the middle of the eighteenth century, the *Bay Psalm Book* was gradually superseded by later developments. The most important of these was published collections of hymns (as well as psalms) in volumes that also offered themselves as instruction manuals on the art of singing. There were good reasons for including these vocal instructions. There is clear evidence of dire concern on the part of New England clergymen in the early eighteenth century that psalm singing was falling into a sad state, especially in the rural areas where the churches might not be able to afford multiple copies of the psalters, or where the congregations might be largely illiterate. In these circumstances the singing of psalms was carried on by rote. The congregation was usually led by the clergyman or a gifted layman who would "line out" the psalms, that is, sing each line alone to introduce it to the congregation and refresh its memory. After the solo statement of each line, the congregation would repeat it. There is aural evidence from the continued practice of rural, illiterate psalm-singing congregations, which to this day still use lining out, to show us what the clergymen were complaining about. In Southern rural congregations, both black and white, we can still hear the same thing: the pace of the singing is slowed down drastically, perhaps to allow for the melodic ornamentation that is interpolated between any two notes anywhere in the tune. The ornamentation itself is the result of the individual singer's perception of melodic necessity, and therefore results in many simultaneous different variations on the tune. In addition, another type of improvisation is going on: more or less talented members of the congregation are improvising different parts (intentionally or unintentionally) above and below the tune, and all this is made even more diversified by the fact that every singer has his own idea of rhythm and tempo. Here is how one Boston clergyman expressed it in 1721:

> For want of exactitude, I have observed in many places one man is upon a note while another a note behind, which produces something hideous and is beyond expression bad. . . .Our tunes are, for want of a Standard to appeal to in all our singing, left to the mercy of every unskilled Throat to chop and alter, twist and change, according to their infinitely divers and no less odd Humors and Fancies.[5]

The clergy were concerned that this "common" method of singing was corrupting the tunes (and more important, the texts) of the psalms beyond recognition.

As a direct result, the Reverend John Tufts in 1721 published a tiny book entitled *An Introduction to the Singing of Psalm-Tunes in a Plain and Easy Method* that prefaces its collection of music with pedagogical remarks on how to read notation, time and key signatures, accidentals, treble and bass "cliff," and so on. This is followed by a few notational illustrations of these necessities, and this in turn by three-part settings (with the tunes in the top part) of thirty-seven psalm tunes, almost all taken from previous sources. By its tiny dimensions (twenty-four pages of less than three by six inches) and pedagogical introduction, it was obviously an attempt to produce a book whose price was within the range of all and whose purpose was to reform "corrupted psalmody."

Having reached the conclusion that traditional notation was an obstacle to correct or "regular" psalm singing, the Reverend Tufts devised a system based on alphabetical letters that he thought would be simpler. As the *Bay Psalm Book* had already been doing for a generation, he used the four letters *f, s, l,* and *m* to represent *fa, sol, la,* and *mi,* but took the further step of placing the letters in their proper places on the five-line staff and adding rhythmic indications (F = $\flat$, F· = $\flat$, F: = $\mathbf{o}$). The resulting system seemed a considerable aid to the advancement of regular psalmody.

But here again we find only four syllables out of the seven we know to have been currently in use in European musical pedagogy. Why? No good reason that satisfies musical logic can

be offered. All that can be said is that the intervals indicated
by *fa sol la* fit the whole-step progressions found in the first
three notes of the major scale as well as intervals of the fourth,
fifth, and sixth notes. The *mi* is used to create the mi-fa or half-
step interval, which is found between the seventh and eighth
degrees of the major scale. Thus an ascending major scale would
be sung fa sol la fa sol la mi fa. The fact that the half-step
occurring between the third and fourth degrees was la-fa and
thus inconsistent with the mi-fa of the seventh and eighth degrees
seemed to offer no problems to anyone. The durability of this
system of four-syllable solfège is impressive: at the end of the
eighteenth century the same pattern of four syllables was used
as the basis for the shape notes that lasted in rural psalmody
and hymnody throughout the nineteenth century, and is still
cultivated by congregations in the South today.

Thus the importance of the Reverend Tufts's 1721 psalter
is that it marks the beginning of the movement to include musical
pedagogy in psalm books, and develops a system of notation
that was to have widespread influence in the following century.

Another movement grew out of clerical concerns for correctness in psalm singing, the singing school. This movement deals
not solely with psalters, hymnbooks, and musical pedagogy,
but introduces a new phenomenon, the American professional
musician. Before the singing-school movement of the mid-
eighteenth century, psalters were written (edited is a more
correct term) by clergymen, and the psalms were sung by congregations. No professional musician played any part in the
process. The first type of American to bear the name musician
(professional or semiprofessional, trained or untrained) appears
in conjunction with the singing-school movement. In urging a
return to "regular psalmody" a Reverend Symmes asks:

Would it not greatly tend to promote singing of psalms if
singing schools were promoted? Would not this be conforming
to the scripture pattern? Have we not as much need of them
as God's people of old? Have we any reason to expect to be
inspired with the gift of singing any more than that of reading?. . .Where would be the difficulty or what the disadvantage
if people who want skill in singing would procure a skillful
person to instruct them, and meet two or three evenings in a
week from 5 or 6 O'Clock to 8, and spend the time in learning
to sing? Would not this be an innocent and profitable recre-

ation and would it not have a tendency, if prudently managed, to prevent the unprofitable expense of time on other occasions? . . .Are they not very unwise who plead against learning to sing by rule, when they can't learn to sing at all unless they learn by rule?[6]

These proposals seem to describe the institutions that soon developed. Directed by itinerant musicians who charged a small fee and promoted their own songbooks, these meetings served not only as ad hoc music schools, but also as social occasions. As can be seen in the pedagogical introductions to the tune books, the curricula of these singing schools were limited to the rudiments of notation and theory with a few admonitions on choral musicianship such as these:

1. In learning the 8 notes, get the Assistance of some Person well acquainted with the Tones and Semitones.
2. Chuse that Part which you can sing with the greatest Ease, and make yourself Master of that first.
3. Sound all high Notes soft as possible, but low ones hard and full.
4. Pitch your Tune so that the highest and lowest Notes may be sounded distinctly.[7]

This advice comes from one of the earliest American publications reflecting the singing-school movement, a 1761 volume by James Lyon called *Urania.* Its lengthy full title refers to new genres and a variety of textures: not only psalm tunes, but also anthems and hymns in two, three, and four parts. The music is engraved in clear, easily read notation in four parts. In Lyon's representation of "Old Hundred," the tune is in the tenor part following the older traditions, but he ignored the innovations of Tufts's *Introduction* and made use of traditional notation. By contrast most of the hymns are in two parts and, when the text is not a psalm known to all, its text is underlain, as it is in a hymn that Lyon names "Salisbury," but which is known today as an Easter hymn named "Lyra Davidica." The anthems are through-composed, extended compositions using a variety of textures and compositional techniques, including sections based on imitative texture, thus introducing contrapuntal independence of line and texture new to the New England Puritan traditions of musical worship. Most of Lyon's psalms, hymns, and anthems are taken from previous sources, so that even though *Urania* represents an early and important source coming out of the singing-school movement, Lyon cannot be called an American composer. That term is best applied to men such as the well-known William Billings (1746-1800), the one-eyed, lame Boston tanner, singing-school teacher, and composer, who was perhaps the first American to devote himself entirely to music as a profession. Billings includes a large number of his own compositions in his six published collections of church music. They reveal him as an appealingly rough-hewn, independent composer whose works have the honest directness that we associate with early New England. Perhaps the best example is his four-part canon "When Jesus Wept."

In this tiny composition we find the simple, direct unsophisticated honesty of expression that places Billings at the head of this early group of American composers. In his later publications Billings did not limit himself to compositions on religious texts, but included some secular pieces, one of which, an anti-British song known as "Chester," became the unofficial anthem of the rebellious colonies in their struggle against England. An example of Billings's unorthodox style can be seen in its four successive parallel fifths between the first and third parts in measures 3 and 4. The text refers to actual events and British generals by name, and makes the entire piece worthy of attention not only as music but also as historical document.

Billings even went so far as to include a comic piece ("Jargon") whose text not only calls for, "Discord as terrible as thunder," which request is naturally fulfilled by the music, but also a concert piece whose text refers to the musical texture of the composition itself ("Let the bass take the lead and firmly proceed till the parts are agreed to fugue away"). Compositions in which imitative counterpoint was the featured texture seem to have been popular among singing-school habitues. They appear in great number and are called *fuging tunes*. A number of scholars think that the pronunciation was "fudge," which may or may not reflect on the musical texture or the choral performance itself. One of the best ways to observe Billings's thinking is to read his prefatory remarks to *The New England Psalm Singer* (1770):

> Perhaps it may expected by some that I should say something concerning rules for composition; to these I answer that nature is the best dictator, for all the hard, dry studied rules that ever was prescribed, will not enable any person to form an air. . . .It must be Nature, Nature must lay the foundation Nature must inspire the thought. . . .For my part, as I don't think myself confined to any rules for composition, laid down by any there were before me, neither should I think. . .that any one who came after me were any ways obligated to adhere to them, any further than they should think proper; so in fact, I think it best for every composer to be his own carver.[8]

It is this very independence, this pride in untutored rejection of European rules (at times verging on cussed orneriness), that returns in glory with Charles Ives to restate the claim that Americans are not simply transplanted Europeans, and that America's music must speak for Americans, and in the process must make its own rules.

Concurrent with the singing-school movement was a great surge of religious revivalism known as the *Great Awakening.* This evangelical movement was the beginning of the American tradition of revivalism, which is very much alive to this day and has been the origin of many powerful influences on all American music, whether sacred or secular, black or white. The Great Awakening dates from about 1735, and spread from Massachusetts throughout the colonies under the influence of the fiery preaching of Jonathan Edwards (1703-1758) and George Whitefield (1714-70). Like all revivalist movements, the theological direction was to shake people out of the religious lethargy produced by self-satisfaction, prosperity, and habitualized worship. The primary emphases were on personal salvation through a second birth, belief in the imminent second coming of Christ, and evidence of faith through personal revelation. All this was manifested by the emotional transformation of the believer, and witnessed by his transformed behavior. The movement affected all sects: Methodists, Congregationalists, Presbyterians, Quakers, Moravians, and Baptists. The Great Awakening placed much more emphasis on the hymn than it did on the psalm, because the hymn had a newly composed text written especially to speak for the emotional condition of the individual believer.

The psalm was felt to be too closely connected with older, less demonstrative forms of worship, which concentrated on group expressions rather than individual transformations. Besides, the psalm was of Old Testament origin, and the Great Awakening concentrated on the New Testament experience.

After the beginning of the nineteenth century, the more settled areas came under the influence of the movements to "improve" the new nation's cultural level and to elevate its primitive state by the importation of more sophisticated European music. The believers in "scientific progress" hoped that the crudities of revivalism would soon pass away and be forgotten, to be replaced by the "more advanced style" of the best continental music. Fortunately for American hymnody, this was not to be. The cultivated centers of the East got their Lowell Mason arrangements; but thanks to the upsurge of revivalism in the camp meetings of the frontier, the crudities of American hymnody did not disappear. They merely moved west, and took up a new way of life.

The first camp meeting seems to have taken place in Logan County, Kentucky, in the summer of 1800. These were outdoor meetings that went on for weeks, and involved dozens of hellfire-and-brimstone preachers, and thousands of people. It was a rough-and-ready Calvinism, catering to the needs of a struggling population whose lives were totally occupied by the concerted effort to stay alive. The camp meeting served as a release from this struggle and a welcome opportunity to "let go" in the company of thousands of other fervent believers. The music that served these meetings was quite obviously not staid, nor was it introspective, nor well rehearsed, nor sung according to the regulations of Eastern urban clerical reformers. It was a continuation of the unfettered "common style" of singing but with none of the Puritan reserve. Thus the main contribution of the camp-meeting movement is not that of a compositional style but of an approach to singing—an unlettered, untutored approach that stems from folk music. This tradition of group singing (often as a concomitant of religious ecstasy) spread to the South where it became the main ingredient of the white and black spiritual and the direct ancestor of the gospel music that is heard among fundamentalist and pentecostal sects today. In fact, in a number of regions of the rural South there still exist congregations and singing societies that intentionally preserve the songs (as well as the actual songbooks) of 150 years ago.

One of the most fascinating aspects of this musical movement is the notation adopted by tune-book compilers in an effort to teach the unlettered and untrained in the shortest possible time. Known as the *shape-note system*, this is the epitome of practical invention on the frontier, and is to American music what the log cabin is to American architecture. The use of shape notes appears precisely at the beginning of the nineteenth century and the identity of its inventor is still in dispute. In "St. Anne's" tune, as it appears in Andrew Wyeth's *Repository of Sacred Music* of 1810, the staffs, clefs, meter, and rhythmic notation are all standard. The only innovation is the shapes of the note-heads. Upon sight-reading a few measures, we might ask what purpose is served by the shapes since all the other musical parameters are obviously notated without ambiguity. To understand the rationale behind shape notes we need to backtrack to the *Bay Psalm Book* and John Tufts's *Introduction to the Singing of Psalm Tunes*. In both these books a system of four solfège syllables (fa, sol, la, and mi) was used to help the singer learn to read: *The Bay Psalm Book* placed the letters f-s-l-m under the staff, while Tufts placed them on it. Shape notes is merely another step along the same path: note-head shapes are used to represent the four syllables (◿= fa, ◯ = sol, ☐ = la, and ◇ = mi) and thus the profusion of alphabetical letters on the staff is eliminated and the hymn can be written in standard rhythmic notation. The syllables were applied to the degrees of the scale in the same pattern followed earlier,

fa	sol	la	fa	sol	la	mi	fa
◿	◯	☐	◿	◯	☐	◇	◿

so that a reading of the "St. Anne's" tune would produce sol-la-la-sol-fa-fa-mi-fa, sol-la-sol-la-fa-sol. The custom was to do just this: Sing the hymn through once with the syllables before going back and singing the text. Shape notes (also known as *patent* notes or *buckwheat* notes) caught on immediately and were utilized in hundreds of collections throughout the nineteenth century. It proved so workable that many compilers tried to extend or improve it to include different shapes for each of the seven notes of the scale. Although such innovations might seem to represent an improvement, and though dozens of different systems were brought forth, the original form of the shape-note system was the only one that lasted.

Of the hundreds of collections printed in the nineteenth century, the most influential were Wyeth's *Repository* (part II, 1813), Walker's *Southern Harmony* (1835), and White and King's *Sacred Harp* (1844). The durability of this last is indicated by the fact that its continued use has required reeditions dated 1911, 1936, and 1967. Part II of Wyeth's *Repository* is the source for many later collections. It is interesting to compare the tune known as "Kedron" from that collection and the same tune as it appears in *Southern Harmony*. Although the tune and its three-part harmonization are obviously the same, the compilers had no qualms about altering rhythms and pitches either to conform to their own traditions of performance or to make it less demanding for the singers. Also interesting are the numerous printer's errors in rhythm and pitch (in the last note of the Wyeth version, F appears instead of E).

With a quick look at this short hymn we can find many of the harmonic and contrapuntal characteristics typical of shape-note settings (and that also are found in the works of William Billings and the eighteenth-century New England composers). These are the very characteristics that give them pioneer strength and innocent beauty, and which at the time earned them the scorn of more sophisticated Eastern and urban reformers. Neither of the last two chords in the first measure contains a third, and on the last chord of the same measure the bass moves down to double the fifth of the triad that with the omitted third makes a particularly odd sonority. In the second measure the two upper parts cross over each other, and the first and last chords of measure three again have no third in them. In measure four the first chord (with fifth lacking) is in first inversion but is "incorrectly" resolved, while the last two chords have no third. In measure five the tune leaps an octave up and crosses over the upper part while the bass takes the third (a more "correct" voice leading would have the bass hold the root while the upper part would move down to the G to take the third of the triad). Parallel fifths occur between top voices in measures five and six. The first chord of measure six has no third, and the first inversion chord on the second beat is "incorrectly" resolved in the bass. The harmonic movement of these same measures exhibits a nightmare of confusion for the analyst who seeks the predictable progressions of functional chord relationships. The setting is in natural minor or the Aeolian mode, but nowhere is a major dominant triad (containing the D-sharp leading tone) introduced to define the key in the functional sense. The first two measures never leave the tonic and the rest of the first phrase moves "illogically" in the area of the VII, VI, and III, and never makes any approach to the V-I progression necessary to define a key according to all the rules of the time. The second phrase has the same characteristics as the first, with the added attraction of a downbeat dissonance of a second on the first syllable of "agony" in measure nine. Is this an intentional depiction of the meaning of the word or not?

Many writers have compared this strange kind of voice leading to medieval organum where many of the same devices are found. The point can be made that, like compositions of the thirteenth century, these tunesmiths (as well as the singers) were not thinking in terms of harmonic progressions and were only interested in the progression of three more or less independent lines. Furthermore, in both types of music the harmonic outlines are further obscured by the phenomenon of any or all of the parts being doubled (or tripled) an octave higher or lower, and by the constant presence of improvised variation and ornamentation of the lines themselves. When we hear any of the many recordings of sacred harp singing of today, we realize that the music lies not in the composition but in the performance.

In this example we see a tune that remains firmly outside the major-minor tonal scheme by staying within the Aeolian mode throughout. Many other tunes are in Dorian, Lydian, Mixolydian, and even the Phrygian modes. In other cases (though not in this one), one finds tunes that omit certain degrees of the scale and the second and/or sixth degrees in a minor scale. These "gapped" or pentatonic scales plus the use of the modes are evidence of the creative influence of folk music at work in the formation of this music.

Dr. George Pullen Jackson, the most noted scholar in the field of Southern American hymnody, divided this music into three categories: 1) religious ballads in which the text relates a biblical narrative, 2) folk hymns in which the text is one of praise, and 3) spiritual songs, whose text most often deals with the trials and anticipated joys of Christian life. All three of these types are likely to use tunes borrowed from secular folk music; and the third type, the spiritual song, has characteristics that relate it to its function origin, the revival camp meeting, since its structure is a direct result of the singing patterns followed at camp meetings. We are informed about these procedures not only from written accounts of 150 years ago but also from the fact that the same procedure is followed today. The song leader and the congregation form the two structural elements of the performing group: the leader guides the progress of the song and introduces the verses in the order he chooses, while the congregation responds to him by picking up his cues and singing the rest of the verse he begins (if they know it), and providing the refrains at the end of the lines.

In "The Good Old Way" from *Southern Harmony* we can see the many stanzas that provide material for an extended performance, plus the congregational hallelujahs at the end of all four lines. Historical accounts tell us that this was not only the way that spiritual songs were learned but also the way they were created—new verses and new tunes being assembled on the spot with congregational refrains liberally applied as the glue to hold the entire structure together.

The strength and durability of this uniquely American type of music is not only shown in its continued cultivation today but also by the fact that it formed the foundation for all American spiritual and gospel music (both white and black) ever since. Perhaps one road toward the further development of American music lies in taking a good look not only at the music of early American hymnody but also at the functional aesthetics that produced it. In this way we might be able to establish our own set of aesthetic criteria with which to judge our own music.

Notes

1. *Boston Handel and Haydn Society Collection of Church Music* (Boston: Richardson and Lord, 1822). Republished by the Music Library Association as no. 15 in the series *Earlier American Music,* ed. H. Wiley Hitchcock (New York, 1973).

2. Gilbert Chase, *America's Music* (New York: McGraw-Hill, 1955), p. 159.

3. H. Wiley Hitchcock, *Music in the United States: A Historical Introduction* (Englewood Cliffs, N.J.: Prentice-Hall, 1969), p. 57.

4. Chase, p. 160.

5. Thomas Walter, *The Grounds and Rules of Musick Explained, or an Introduction to the Art of Singing by Note* (Boston, 1721).

6. Rev. Thomas Symmes, *The Reasonableness of Regular Singing, or Singing by Note* (Boston, 1720).

7. Rev. James Lyon, *Urania, A Choice Collection of Psalm-Tunes, Anthems, and Hymns, From the most approv'd Authors, with some Entirely New; in Two, Three, and Four Parts. The whole Peculiarly adapted to the Use of Churches, and Private Families: To which are Prefix'd The Plainest, & most Necessary Rules of Psalmody* (Philadelphia, 1761. Republished, New York: DaCapo Press, 1974).

8. William Billings, *The New England Psalm Singer* (Boston, 1770). Quoted from Chase, p. 140.

Illustrations

For further information and other graphics helpful to this chapter see:

Music in America, An Anthology from the Landing of the Pilgrims to the Close of the Civil War, 1620-1865, edited by Thomas W. Morrocco and Harold Gleason (New York: Norton, 1964).

Repository of Sacred Music, Second Part, Second ed., edited by Andrew Wyeth (New York: Da Capo Press, 1964).

The Southern Harmony, edited by William Walker (Philadelphia: Pro Musica American, 1966).

4

Charles Ives's Optimism: or, The Program's Progress

Roy V. Magers

In considering what is "American" in this country's music, one can hardly refrain from particular mention of the music of Charles Ives. To be sure, whatever is American in Ives's music is no single, simple thing. In its very complexity and diversity lie part of its national quality and its value for people who would understand that quality. Ives and his music still leave many unanswered questions, and any exploration of the problems they pose has a potential for illuminating some of the varied strands that weave the tangled web of America's music(s).

The very coexistence in Ives's music of such seeming opposites as the naive and the sophisticated, the vernacular and the cultivated, the traditional and the avant-garde, the urban and the rural, the obvious and the obscure, and the clear and the distorted is perhaps ultimately more revealing of Ives and his Americanness than it is perplexing, if taken as symbolic of both his acceptance and rejection of numerous aspects of his multifaceted European-American musical, intellectual, cultural, and social heritage. Indeed, a picture of the man has recently emerged that reveals him to have been not only the astonishingly powerful, original, and independent creator he has long been generally acknowledged to have been, but also one who was profoundly influenced, both positively and negatively, consciously and unconsciously, in myriad and subtle ways, by several forces in the complex of his inherited musical-cultural life.[1]

Recognizing that "The Case of Mr. Ives" (with a bow to Elliot Carter's 1939 *Modern Music* article) is by no means a simple one, and that it cannot be explained by any one of the external forces that molded him (or even by a combination of them), I would like to focus some attention on just one of his characteristic attitudes that lies at the very core of his existence as an American individual and composer. I speak of Ives's optimism.

It is clear that an underlying optimism in the progress of human existence pervades much of Ives's prose. This same faith seems also to have exerted a significant influence on the formation of some of his music, where it is expressed primarily through associative means, by words of songs and hymns whose tunes Ives so liberally quoted in his works. It finds perhaps its fullest display in what appears to be a kind of sub rosa literary program to the *Fourth Symphony*, suggested by hymns associated with quoted tunes, where the image of the religious Pilgrim seeking God and at last finding Him may be interpreted as a symbol of a belief that an ultimate good, which is the goal of all human life, will eventually be achieved by man.

Throughout a large part of Ives's prose essays is expressed an abiding faith in mankind and in man's spiritual development and progress, which will lead one day to a state of near-perfection of life on earth. Entailed in this faith is the belief that, no matter how bad things seem or really are at any time, this ideal state will be the final outcome of the future. The chief instrument for the attainment of this goal is the innate goodness of humankind itself, a goodness that is the manifestation of the essentially spiritual, universal quality of all existence. This is the tenor of much of the *Essays Before a Sonata* and in particular of the essay entitled "The Majority." In a very condensed and simplified form, it is expressed in the words of the song, "Majority":

> The Masses! The Masses!
> The Masses have toiled,
> Behold the works of the World!
> The Masses are thinking,

Whence comes the thought of the World!
The Masses are singing,
Whence comes the Art of the World!
The Masses are yearning,
Whence comes the hope of the World!
The Masses are dreaming,
Whence come the visions of God!
God's in His Heaven,
All will be well with the World![2]*

This sentiment should lead no one to suspect that Ives was a pollyanna. He knew well enough the reasons for pessimism and was thoroughly angered by the atrocities of war and politics in the world. But his overall outlook seems to have been close to that which he ascribed to Emerson:

If Emerson must be dubbed an optimist—then an optimist fighting pessimism, but not wallowing in it; an optimist who does not study pessimism by learning to enjoy it; whose imagination is greater than his curiosity; who, seeing the signpost to Erebus is strong enough to go the other way.[3]

While Ives's own optimism was based on the strong conviction that eventually "all will be well with the world," it recognized that the immediate future was often uncertain and unpredictable. For example, in speculating about what might happen in both the short and the long run if the power Ives thought the majority (the masses) should have were actually given to it, he asks:

Why not make a start, if it is only to find out if a start is wanted! Why not ask this Majority giant, this great mass personality, if he is willing to sit for a trial portrait before the world's most critical artist—even himself?
And what will the picture be? Hideous or transcendent? A caricature or a Velasquez? At its birth, or in its youth? We know not. But as it approaches maturity, there will come, we believe, a radiance such as the world has never seen!
"Why! Why!" the Pilgrims turn and ask.
Man knows not the horizon of the soul—but Faith has yet its Olivet, and Love its Galilee![4]

This faith in and concern for ultimate conclusions may be partly reflected in Ives's awareness of the importance of endings in prose, poetry, and music. For example, in "Essays Before a Sonata," he speaks of Emerson's "codas" that "seem to crystallize in a dramatic though serene and sustained way the truths of his subject—they become more active and intense, but quieter and deeper"[5]; and of the "underlying courage of the purest humility that gives Emerson the outward aspect of serenity which is felt to so great extent in much of his work, especially in his codas and perorations."[6]

Ives's consciousness of the possibility that a conclusion could crystallize the essential meaning of that which had preceded it is further demonstrated in his witty introductory comments to "Romanzo di Central Park":

Leigh Hunt, in his Essays, "Rhyme and Reasons," says:. . . "yet how many 'poems' are there. . .of which we require no more than the rhymes, to be acquainted with the whole of them? You know what the rogues have done by the ends they come to. For instance, what is more necessary to inform us of all the following gentleman has for sale, than the bell he tinkles at the end of his cry? We are as sure of him as the muffin-man." Then he quotes the beautiful text, found in the song below. It is called a "Love Song," but that is not enough; when attached to music, it becomes a "Morceau du Coeur,"— a "Romanzo di Central Park," or an "Intermezzo Table d'hote." Was there ever peroration more eloquent? Ever a series of catastrophes more explanatory of their previous history?[7]

In some of Ives's music it seems probable that conclusions are meant to play a role somewhat analogous to the "end rhymes" of the Hunt poem that is the text of "Romanzo di Central Park" ("Grove, Rove, Night, Delight. . ."). The "meaning" and "previous history" that they "explain" is a programmatic one revealed partially throughout a composition by musical quotations and the texts associated with them, and brought to a positive end by the final part of the work, which presents the concluding quotation or quotations. In the Fourth Symphony, the esoteric programmatic structure thus created may be taken to symbolize man's spiritual progress, in Christian symbols that depict the soul's quest for union with God—the final goal of a good life.

The essential details of Henry Bellamann's account in 1927 (approved by Ives) of that work's program are already well known. Its central theme is "the searching questions of What? and Why? which the spirit of man asks of life."[8] The central image evoked by texts associated with quoted hymn tunes is that of the wandering Pilgrim seeking his way toward the heavenly home. His journey seems to symbolize those searching questions and "the diverse answers in which existence replies."[9] The general outline of this program may be sketched as follows: In the "First Movement," the Pilgrim asks for signs of assurance that his journey will end successfully; in the "Second Movement," he makes a false start by traveling on the devilish and illusory "Celestial Railroad"; in the "Third Movement," he catches glimpses of a vision of his true destination and the means for reaching it; in the "Fourth Movement," the goal of the journey—now known to be God himself—is neared. There is no assurance that the goal is actually reached, but it seems certain that it eventually will be. The fading away of the coda into a kind of "silence of eternity" strengthens these feelings.

Excerpts from Bellamann's program will provide a frame of reference for the expositon of that more detailed program that Ives may have had in mind, and intended to evoke associatively through his use of hymn-tune quotations:

This symphony. . .consists of four movements—a Prelude, a majestic fugue, a third movement in comedy vein, and a finale of transcendental spiritual content. The aesthetic program of the work is. . .the searching questions of What? and Why? which the spirit of man asks of life. This is particularly the sense of the prelude. The three succeeding movements are the diverse answers in which existence replies. . . .The fugue . . .is an expression of the reaction of life into formalism and ritualism. The succeeding movement. . .is not a scherzo. . . .It is a comedy in the sense that Hawthorne's *Celestial Railroad* is comedy. Indeed this work of Hawthorne's may be considered as a sort of incidental program in which an exciting, easy, and worldly progress through life is contrasted with the trials of the Pilgrims in their journey through the swamp. The occasional slow episodes—Pilgrims' hymns—are constantly crowded out and overwhelmed by the former. The dream, or fantasy, ends with an interruption of reality—the Fourth of July in Concord—brass bands, drum corps, etc. . . .[10]

To this must be appended a later addition to Bellamann's program made by Ives: "In a way, as stated in Mr. Bellamann's program notes, 'The last movement is an apotheosis of the preceding, in terms that have something to do with the reality of existence and its religious experience.' "[11]

The motif of the Pilgrim is presented in the "First Movement" by the tune "Watchman," whose hymn text is a dialogue between a traveler and a watchman in which the traveler asks what the signs of promise are for his journey. Portions of texts associated with other tunes quoted in the "First Movement" also may be related to the travel image: The introduction alludes to "In the Sweet By and By" and "Bethany" ("Nearer, My God, to Thee"), which may be taken to suggest that the "promised land" or God Himself is the ultimate goal of the journey. Simultaneously presented with "Watchman" are "Proprior Deo" and "Something for Thee." It is noteworthy that one hymn text set to "Proprior Deo" in Ives's time was also "Nearer, My God, to Thee,"[12] and that one verse of "Something for Thee" ("Saviour, Thy Dying Love") speaks of "some wanderer sought and won."

Fragments of "Nettleton" also appear in the "First Movement," and some of its stanzas speak of a wanderer or of a journey toward a heavenly home:

Here I raise my Ebenezer,
Hither by Thy help I'm come;
And I hope by Thy good pleasure,
Safely to arrive at home.
[. . .]
Jesus sought me when a stranger,
Wand'ring from the fold of God;
He, to rescue me from danger,
Interposed His precious blood.

Either a journey, a wanderer or traveler, arrival in heaven, or all three are mentioned in portions of hymn texts associated with the tunes quoted. Similar associations can be observed in other movements.

The program of the "Second Movement" is, as suggested in the Bellamann-Ives program, closely related to Hawthorne's *The Celestial Railroad*, a parody of Bunyan's *Pilgrim's Progress*. Several musical events and sounds parallel the story's scenario. The movement has as major components the two metaphorical motifs of the journey and the dream. As general structure, the dream metaphor provides a context within which rapid shifts of mood and multilayered action have their own logic. As a structure with specific content, the fantasy contains evocations of various events in Hawthorne's story, including the Pilgrims' slow hymns, the Pilgrims' "trials in their journey through the swamp," and the contrasting "exciting, easy, and worldly progress through life."[13]

Certain portions of some hymn tunes used in the movement seem to comment on the program's (and the Pilgrims') progress. Particularly striking are tunes whose texts speak of a promised land: "Beulah Land" and "In the Sweet By and By" ("There's a Land that is fairer than day") are the principal tunes, and "There Is a Happy Land" also appears briefly but significantly. Certain verses of the quoted hymn tunes also suggest a promised land or final home and resting place. The relevant part of "Nettleton" 's words has already been mentioned, and the last stanza of the first verse of "Martyn," which appears simultaneously with a nearly complete statement of "Beulah Land" toward the movement's conclusion says, "Safe into the haven guide; O receive my soul at last!" It is also significant that while the verse of "In the Sweet By and By" appears in several places in the movement, its refrain is stated only in the loud climax that immediately precedes the statement of "Beulah Land," which is the goal—both musical and programmatic—of the main portion of the movement (the dream). The words of this refrain are: "In the sweet By and By, we shall meet on that beautiful shore." (In *The Celestial Railroad*, as well as in Bunyan's *Pilgrim's Progress*, the Celestial City is bordered by a river.)

"Beulah Land" 's text further comments on the arrival of both the true and false pilgrims at the goal of their journey:

> I've reached the land of corn and wine,
> And all its riches freely mine;
> Here shines undimmed one blissful day,
> For all my night has passed away,
>
> O Beulah Land, sweet Beulah Land,
> As on thy highest mount I stand,
> I look away across the sea,

Where mansions are prepared for me,
And view the shining glory-shore—
My Heav'n, my home forevermore.

This is played in conjunction with "Martyn" ("O recieve my soul
at last!'").

But the soul is not yet received. In the interruption of
reality that intrudes upon the end of "Beulah Land," part of
the text of "Turkey in the Straw" (one of several secular
tunes in that portion of the movement) seems too closely related
to Hawthorne's story for coincidence: "I came to the river, and
I couldn't get across. . . ."

In the "Third Movement," indications of a progressive un-
folding of a program evoked by hymn-tune quotations are not
evident. The publicly stated programmatic theme (the "reaction
of life into formalism and ritualism") seems to be suggested
mainly by the movement's "academic" fugal texture. Textual
imagery appears to be vague and tenuous, but there are connections among hymn texts that may be more than coincidental.
Of the four borrowed tunes in the movement ("Missionary
Hymn," "Coronation," "Welcome Voice," and "Antioch"), all
but "Welcome Voice" speak of Christ as the reigning king.
Perhaps the hymn that "Welcome Voice" most commonly sets
("I hear Thy welcome voice") is at least externally related to
the one usually associated with "Coronation" ("All hail the
power of Jesus' name!") by the fact that three lines of one of
the former's stanzas begin with the acclamation, "All hail!"

The theme of travel is presented by "Missionary Hymn,"
but it is not the journey of a seeker. Rather, it is the journey of
one called to spread abroad a truth that is considered to be
already attained and finished (a "reaction into formalism"?):

From Greenland's icy mountains,
From India's coral strand;
Where Afric's sunny fountains
Roll down their golden sand:
From many an ancient river,
From many a palmy plain,
They call us to deliver
Their land from error's chain.

More centrally related to the images spoken of earlier and to the ones found at the end of the movement, however, is another hymn text sometimes set to "Missionary Hymn" in Ives's day that possibly he could have known and have had in mind—not necessarily to the exclusion of any others:

> The morning light is breaking, the darkness disappears;
>   [. . .]
> Blest river of salvation, Pursue the onward way;
> Flow thou to every nation, Nor in thy richness stay;
> Stay not till all the lowly Triumphant reach their home;
> Stay not till all the holy Proclaim, "The Lord is come."[14]

That Ives may well have been thinking of this latter hymn when he decided to include this movement in the symphony is indicated by ideas and words connected with the two tunes he added at the movement's conclusion, tunes not quoted in the original version for string quartet: "Welcome Voice" and "Antioch." "Antioch" 's most commonly used hymn begins, "Joy to the World, the Lord is Come!" Though the portion of the tune that sets these words is not quoted, any reference to it at all might evoke a memory of the hymn's well-known opening words. The words to the quoted refrain of "Welcome Voice" are, "I am coming Lord, Coming home to Thee." The juxtaposition of these tunes, which coincide with the only presentation in the movement of "Missionary Hymn" 's last phrase ("Stay not till all the holy proclaim, 'The Lord is come' " in the setting of "The Morning Light Is Breaking"), suggests a reciprocal "journey" on the part of man and God: each comes to meet the other. The fact that these associations can be made with tunes added by Ives to only the *Fourth Symphony* version of this movement indicates a conscious attempt to link the movement programmatically by means of hymn-tune quotations with other movements.

Images expressed by certain texts associated with principal quotations in the "Fourth Movement" indicate that the goal of the Pilgrim's search—union with God—is close at hand. Not all of these are the hymns most commonly associated with the tunes quoted, but all could have been known to Ives. (Whether he actually knew them or not is, of course, an open question.) The hymns that are normally set to the principal tunes Ives used are: "Dorrnance" ("Saviour Who Thy flock art feeding"); "Missionary Chant" ("Ye Christian Heralds, go proclaim" and, "Asleep in Jesus!"); "Martyn" ("Jesus, Lover of my soul"); "St. Hilda" ("O Jesus, Thou art standing outside the fast-closed door" and, "A Pilgrim and a stranger, I journey here below"); and "Bethany" ("Nearer, My God, to Thee").[15] All these hymns make some reference to a heavenly home, a final resting place, a spiritual journey, or coming closer to God. The number of common images to be found in these texts is remarkable. The themes they express are, of course, very central to fundamental Christian belief and are widespread in "gospel" and mainstream Protestant hymnody. In spite of this, the number of correspondences among them seem too great for mere coincidence.

Two of these hymns deserve special mention because of their close relationship to the central images of the symphony: "A Pilgrim and a Stranger" (set to "St. Hilda") and "Nearer, My God, to Thee" (set to "Bethany"). "St. Hilda" and "Bethany" are among the last-quoted tunes in the symphony: "St. Hilda" appears embedded in a web of complex thematic simultaneity that includes "Dorrnance," "Missionary Chant," and "Martyn"; "Bethany" provides the principal thematic material of the coda of the movement. The words most commonly associated with "St. Hilda" are appropriate enough in the context of the covert program I am suggesting, and may well have been the only ones Ives had in mind, since this text reinforces the notion of the reciprocal journey of man and Christ evoked at the end of the "Third Movement," and paints a picture of immediate anticipation of the ultimate union of God and man:

> O Jesus, Thou art standing
> 　　outside the fast-closed door,
> In lowly patience waiting
> 　　to pass the threshold o'er
> 　　　　　[. . .]
> O Lord with shame and sorrow
> 　　we open now the door.
> Dear Saviour enter, enter,
> 　　and leave us nevermore!

But "A Pilgrim and a Stranger," set to "St. Hilda" in Melancthon Stryker's *Church Praise Book* of 1888, so strikingly recapitulates all the central imagery mentioned thus far that it is difficult to believe that Ives was not thinking of that text, too:

A Pilgrim and a stranger,
   I journey here below;
Far distant is my country,
   the home to which I go:
Here must I toil and travail,
   oft weary and oppressed,
But there my God shall lead me
   to everlasting rest.[16]

Portions of "Nearer, My God, to Thee" also refer to a traveler and to a hoped-for, final resting place with God. The refrain of its tune ("Bethany") is the main melodic material for the work's conclusion, thus suggesting that the Pilgrim's journey is nearly over:

Though like the wanderer, the sun gone down,
Darkness be over me, my rest a stone:
Yet in my dreams I'd be nearer, my God, to Thee,
Nearer, my God, to Thee, nearer to Thee.

Then, with my waking thoughts bright with Thy praise,
Out of my stony griefs, Bethel I'll raise;
So by my woes to be nearer, my God, to Thee,
Nearer, my God, to Thee, Nearer to Thee!

The programmatic goal of the Pilgrim's union with God is underscored by the musical goal of the return of a firm, yet clouded, tonal center of D, absent since its disappearance at the end of the "First Movement." And, as the words of the hymn leave just a little to be desired (the union is nowhere actually described as completed), the music also ends on a mildly inconclusive note—only the faint sounds of the percussion battery unit are left to overhang the strings, which have already faded away into silence. The implication seems to be that Ives thought of the substratum of percussion sound that permeates the movement as a kind of eternal, ongoing life force, like that of "earth's motion and pulse" in the percussion unit of the projected "Universe Symphony."[17]

Such a musical termination may remind us of Emerson's "codas" that became "quieter and deeper" and seemed to "crystallize in a dramatic though serene way the truths of his subject." Perhaps we may attribute to Ives the attitude toward his work's "message" that Ives believed Emerson had concerning his—that he was "conscious of its vagueness but ever hopeful for it, and confident that its foundation, if not its medium, is somewhere near the eventual and absolute good—the divine truth underlying all life."[18]

It seems clear that Ives did indeed intend the *Fourth Symphony* and especially its last movement to "have something to do with the reality of existence and its religious experience." In that religious experience was summed up and symbolized for Ives the best that man could hope for and a promise that it could and would be attained. But not without effort. The true Pilgrim must "toil and travail, oft weary and oppressed," but he will be rewarded for his labors by the fruition of the seed of innate goodness within him—by his final and complete union with the ultimate good. This conception of the Pilgrim's (the majority's) mission and of the complementary journey and sacrifice on the part of both man and God is tersely summarized in Ives's song, "The Innate" (words by Ives):

Voices live in every finite being; often undivined, near silence.
Hear them! Hear them in you! in others!
They sense truth deep in all life; they know the things true
    Pilgrims stand for.
Stand out! Come to Him without the things the world brings;
    come to him!
As a child and as a poor man. He had all, He gave all.[19]*

The image of the religious Pilgrim, who undergoes severe trials and tribulations in his journey but comes at last to a sure and glorious union with God, seems a metaphor for the way Ives viewed all of life. The path through it is often obscure and full of obstacles, but its outcome, both on Earth and in heaven, is somewhere near an absolute good. However vague the meaning of the details of life, they point to the "undercurrent of all," which is that eventual good. Is such optimism misguided? We may not know. But we can perhaps share in Ives's American dream that "some morning glorious (but not quite tomorrow) the trend up the mountain resounding around the world will bring a new and radiant horizon to all."[20]

---

*The Innate—From Nineteen Songs, Copyright © 1935,
Merion Music, Inc.; used by permission.

Notes

1. In recent years several people have contributed significantly to an understanding of Ives, the man and the musician. Especially enlightening and provocative are Rosalie Sandra Perry's *Charles Ives and the American Mind* (Kent, Ohio: Kent State University Press, 1974), and Frank Rossiter's *Charles Ives and His America* (New York: Liveright, 1975). Both these studies brilliantly examine the relationships of Ives with his complex American culture from quite different perspectives. Also of inestimable value are Vivian Perlis's oral history, *Charles Ives Remembered* (New Haven, Conn.: Yale University Press, 1974), and John Kirkpatrick's exemplary edition of Ives's *Memos* (New York: Norton, 1972). In addition to these, numerous dissertations and theses have enormously enriched the possibilities for a comprehensive understanding of Ives's musical works and practices.

2. Charles Ives, "Majority," *Nineteen Songs* (Bryn Mawr, Penn.: Merion Music, Inc./Theodor Presser Co., 1935), pp. 38-42.

3. Charles Ives, "Essays Before a Sonata," *Essays Before a Sonata, The Majority, and Other Writings,* ed. Howard Boatwright (New York: Norton, 1970), p. 14.

4. Ives, "The Majority," *Essays Before a Sonata, The Majority, and Other Writings,* ed. Howard Boatwright (New York: Norton, 1970), p. 199.

5. Ives, "Essays," p. 25.

6. Ives, "Essays," pp. 35-36.

7. Charles Ives, Introduction to "Romanzo di Central Park," *Fourteen Songs* (New York: Peer International, n.d.), p. 14.

8. Charles Ives, *Symphony no. 4,* with a preface by John Kirkpatrick (New York: Associated Music Publishers, 1965), p. 8.

9. Ibid.

10. Ibid.

11. Ives, *Memos,* p. 66.

12. *The Hymnal* (Philadelphia: The Presbyterian Board of Publications and Sabbath School Work, 1895), no. 602. Note: Sources for familiar hymn texts commonly associated with tunes quoted and readily available in several modern hymnals are not cited in this chapter.

13. Ives, *Symphony no. 4,* p. 8.

14. *The Church Praise Book,* eds. Melancthon W. Stryker and Hubert P. Main (New York: Biglow and Main, 1888), p. 622.

15. Sources for hymns not ordinarily associated in present-day hymnals with some of these quoted tunes are: *The Presbyterian Hymnal* (Philadelphia: Presbyterian Board of Education, 1867), no. 162 ("Asleep in Jesus"), and no. 526 ("Saviour, who Thy flock art feeding"); and *The Church Praise Book,* ed. Stryker and Main, p. 422 ("A Pilgrim and a Stranger").

16. *The Church Praise Book*, p. 422.

17. Ives, *Memos*, p. 125.

18. Ives, "Essays Before a Sonata," p. 14.

19. Ives, "The Innate," *Nineteen Songs*, pp. 16-17.

20. Charles Ives, "A People's World Nation," *Essays Before A Sonata, The Majority, and Other Writings*, ed. Howard Boatwright (New York: Norton, 1970).

5

The Other Side of
Black Music

Kenneth B. Billups

Some categories of Afro-American music have come to be
regarded as established contributions to American entertainment. In recent years they have been considered as well for their
ethnic-cultural values, and thus have made inroads via our educational institutions.

The American layman usually thinks of jazz, and the sub-
titles of ragtime, urban blues, and hard rock, as the music
attributed to black creativity. Scores of books about these
categories are available. Since music has a developmental stage,
most authors begin with a cursory mention of African roots, and
some elementary discourse is given to blues and spirituals to
give some authoritative urgency to these popular musical expressions. I do not wish to demean this normal approach, for it
is rational in the mind of the writer if the popular categories are
to be pursued.

What frequently happens is that the music of American
blacks and their total contribution to the American scene is not
placed in proper perspective simply because some categories that
are highly entertaining and educationally worthwhile are lost in
the shuffle. Another cause of confusion is the lumping of all

Afro-American religious music into one catchall category termed
gospel music, much as the word *soul* is utilized to indicate in-
definitive indigenous virtuosity exhibited by a performer. This
confusion exists among the spirituals, the gospel songs, and the
use of hymns. A few hymns were written by composers of Afro-
American lineage, but many, composed by English hymn writers,
were stylized with inflections and embellishments that are now
time honored by their use in black churches. These hymns can
easily be identified with proper credits should one peruse the
Baptist hymnal published by the National Convention Organization, with offices at Nashville, Tennessee. Some spirituals are
included in these books, but to add to the confusion many publishers have simply credited certain compositions to the category
"spirituals."

LININ' DR. WATTS

In 1619 a Dutch vessel landed twenty African blacks at
Jamestown, with the rhythms and inherent melodies of Africa
throbbing in their hearts. These people adjusted to the new-found
religion of Christianity, and learned the words of famous hymn
writers of Europe as they sat in the balconies of Eastern
churches. To these words they placed their melodies in call-and-
response form, and these indigenous incantations have lasted
in the black churches for more than 300 years. They can be
heard in most country churches where there is no instrument,
and often in urban churches during a "testimonial" service, or
before a Sunday prayer meeting or afternoon service.

Spirituals are religious Afro-American folk songs, created
by blacks during slavery, principally by camp-meeting gatherings, in the fields to pass the time (just as were field blues),
and often sung long into the night around plantation cabins.
They were passed around, unaccompanied, by rote singing
throughout the Southland, and the most popular of these
survived.

Spirituals appear to fall in three phases, according to the
psychological fixations of the black mind under extreme duress
and the socioreligious conditions of slavery.

The slave trade in the South was substantially rooted around
mid-century. The enslaved people were far from being a part of
the American dream of new freedoms. It is a strange phenom-

enon that throughout the ages people under conditions of forced servitude have created unusual folk music that not only survives but contributes to the cultural development of larger forms in this art. So it is with the American black.

The first phase of the spiritual was preceded by a conglomerate of several characteristics that developed from the field hollers. Initially slaves were not allowed to communicate openly in the field, but could do so by the use of African words or nonverbal musical phrases resembling the call-and-response style of the African boat song. The musical phrase was similar to early European plain chant, but different in melodic structure, utilizing with inflections the two pentatonic African scales now identified with the Western and sub-Sahara African regions. Finally, this was intuitively fused into one scale, which to this day is clearly defined in the musical-scale patterns of Afro-American music.

The initial spirituals consisted of, in the main, a single vocal line with a harmonic background reinforced by octaves, fourths, and fifths in homophonic style (much like early Western organum), but suitably placed in proper perspective and authentically supported as a derivative of many legendary folk songs of Africa. Many of these songs were not entirely religious in word content, but did have punctuated expressions of the Diety: "Oh Lord." The English dialect of the South was second class as conveyed by the white population, and by the time it reached the ear of the slave unfamiliar with a new language, it was not only distorted but also conveyed in simple expressions and dotted with African words. Several authorities on American ethnomusicology subscribe to the belief that the references made to "heaven" in the early religious songs refer to the African homeland, since the early slaves were not privy to religious instruction in the South. Examples of this era include songs like, "Oh I can't stay away, / I wish I had died in Egypt land," and, "Kum Bah Yah, Mah Lord," which is an obvious misreading of the Southern dialectical expression of the words, "Come by Here, My Lord."

Painful as it is to the social thought of the American dream, the spirituals created in the second phase of slavery were most prolific and productive, for it was in this era that the American black lost all hope of regaining freedom. Most songs from this era communicate the sorrowful recognition that the only escape from servitude was by way of heaven as it related to the new-found religion, Christianity. Heroes of the Bible sustained the slaves' belief in a "better day a cumin'," and these heroes are expressed in song, with the principal character being "Jesus" in most songs.

The black used the modes of travel known in that day and analogous to his thinking in the words of spirituals like "Swing Low, Sweet *Chariot*," "Dis *Train* Don' Carry Backsliders," "Sing a-Ho, Dat Ah Had de *Wings* of a Dove," " 'Tis de Ol' *Ship* o' Zion," "*Run* to de Rock," and "Deep *River*." All these songs carry the underlying connotation, consciously or unconsciously, "I'd rather be dead, / Go to heaven, / Than exist in this hellish state."

The camp meeting, supported by the growing belief in heroes of the Bible who had succeeded against odds, and by the compassion of Jesus, who "died for them also," was a positive text suggested in many spirituals: "Go Down Moses," "Ezekiel Saw de Wheel," "Elijah Rock," "Jacob's Ladder," "Story of the Twelve," "Jesus Is a Rock in a Weary Lan'," "Nobody Knows (Like Jesus)," and countless others, numbering over 200 folk songs.

Talk of the abolition of slavery in the early 1800s produced spirituals that related to emancipation, in the third phase. Freedom songs that were direct and indirect in word content were created: "No More Auction Block," "Oh, Freedom," "Slavery Chain Done Broke," or "Free At Last."

Mention should be made of an unusual practice that developed in the camp-meeting era, and still prevails in some of the black churches. The exhortation sermon is often predicated on a text very familiar to the preacher, in which he exhorts in a demonstrative and musically repetitive manner, with the background furnished by the congregation as they "Line Dr. Watts," or sing a spiritual appropriate to the text. It is not only an exciting experience to view and hear but it can and does also produce a sincere religious mass hysteria among the participants. It is a part of ethnic Americana that speaks directly to a cultural experience.

Exciting also are the "praise songs" or "jubilees" that carry with them the natural rhythms so often attributed to the Afro-American. These are spirituals that in their initial form did not carry such terraced rhythms. They were developed by the younger folk who remained after camp meeting to explore these melodies for the purpose of release via body rhythms and dancing. These songs continue to be enjoyed by most high-school and college choirs, and provide for the listener moments of entertainment in our present-day culture.

Special mention should be made of a spiritual that has received one-sided treatment. It is popular and known to most Americans because of its being featured by Louis Armstrong and dixieland jazz bands. These players know the tradition, but many Americans do not.

"When De Saints Go Marchin' In" is a funeral spiritual, and when performed in a church by soloist, congregation, or choir, it is one of the most moving experiences of a plaintive folk song on record. One must share first the vocal experience to fully appreciate the band coming back from the graveyard in the joyous mood of, "One more soul gone to heaven."

SECULAR AFRO-AMERICAN FOLK TUNES

If we are to consider "the other side of black music," we must take note of the nonreligious music created by blacks in an era of oppression. Some of these songs are joyous to relieve the surrounding tension, while others follow an intense feeling of depression. Some of these have remained as simple folk tunes that defy development because of their character, while others have given vent to continued experimentation by black and white musicians, especially in this century. These are the hollers, field blues, work songs, dance songs, legendary hero and folk-tale songs, love songs, Creole songs of all types, and freedom songs. Later are the street cries from the urban areas of the South and convict songs of the chain gangs.

Out of the inception of the holler, and running concurrently with the early spiritual, came another category of secular music known as *field blues* or *rural blues*. This music differs from the urban blues of a much later date, and identifies with them only in relationship to a later development in which they were used as vehicles on the black vaudeville stage.

The scorching heat of the sun and the long dreary hours of work in the field produced songs created on the spot, sometimes intelligible only to the purveyor. Out of this experience came a unitary ballad blues, which has lost some of its significance in the world of black music. But a second three-strain form came out of the field and took root. It was a short, twelve-measure song with the first strain of four measures presenting a sorrowful statement. This is followed by a parallel statement with possible embellishments according to the songster's feeling, and the "pay-off" line suggests a resolution to the problem. Several such verses are repeated with different words until the song-story is complete. Field blues are important to our American music scene because the text contributes to a sharing of individual, everyday problems in an intimate way. The blues were enhanced by the addition of guitar or piano accompaniment or both; other instruments added were the drum, trumpet, and saxophone, according to taste.

This music became popular during the days of black vaudeville, and reached peak level in the taverns and show houses frequented by blacks from 1920 to 1940. It is still an important adjunct to the small band with solo singer, even the hard-rock bands. One who wishes to hear examples of three-strain field blues in their elementary stage can do so on Folkways records, and the development of this form with instrumentation on records by Ma Rainey and Bessie Smith.

SECULAR JUBILEES

A part of the musical heritage of the American black has been a group of folk tunes that sprang from the antebellum period and spilled over into the twentieth century. Many of these were accompanied by body rhythms and dancing. Jubilee songs like the "Hambone" song could go on for hours if there was a crowd and suitable soloists to make up the verses. The same was true of the familiar "Raise the Ruckus Tonite" event, which also employed homemade instruments such as bones, banjos, and tambours. The spontaneity and extemporizing of the music made in front of the cabins and later in urban gathering places, accompanied by dancing, has been described by witnesses as high spirited and entertaining.

THE BLACK RENAISSANCE PERIOD (CIRCA 1905-1940)

It is difficult to place a beginning date on this fruitful era in black music. Although it is somewhat close in years to analogous writing and painting, some productive strides had already been made in black renaissance music by 1905. Will Marion Cook had written *Clorindy*, and had inserted the well-known cakewalk in the late 1800s. A chorus from this show called "Swing Along" was later published by G. Schirmer. Scott Joplin was already on the scene with his piano rags. Two brothers, James Weldon and J. Rosamond Johnson, had written the highly regarded "Lift Ev'ry Voice and Sing," later adopted by several black national organizations as their rallying song. This went to press in 1905.

It was during this period that C. Albert Tindley, Thomas A. Dorsey, and Lucie Campbell wrote gospel songs that live in the black church today. The sophisticated arrangement of spirituals by John W. Work, Harry T. Burleigh, Hall Johnson, Edward Boatner, J. Rosamond Johnson, and Florence Price signaled the entrance of learned musicians on the scene who retained a respect for their heritage. The careers of fine soloists such as Roland Hayes, Paul Robeson, Marian Anderson, and Dorothy Maynor were made secure by their success on the concert stage. Of extreme importance is the fact that many of the arrangements are still published today. Spirituals for chorus were arranged in excellent taste during this period by William A. Dawson of Tuskegee fame. R. Nathaniel Dett not only arranged spirituals for performance with his Hampton Institute Choir, but extended the idiom to anthem form as well. He wrote a cantata entitled *Chariot Jubilee* and an oratorio called *The Ordering of Moses*. John W. Work II of Fisk University wrote the prize-winning cantata based on Longfellow's poem, *The Singers*. It was during this era that Major N. Clark Smith wrote a stunning work for chorus and orchestra called *The Negro Choral Symphony*. William Grant Still, known to many as the "dean of black composers," is principally known as a writer of large instrumental forms. However, his ballet with chorus and orchestra called *Sadhji* connects African roots in story and song in a most admirable fashion.

Clarence Cameron White's opera *Ouanga*, based on the lives of Toussaint L'Ouverture and Dessalines, was completed at the end of this era, though not performed until 1950.

At the end of the black renaissance, spirituals, reminiscent of slavery, fell into ill repute among many people of color in their quest for first-class citizenship in America. It was not until the push and exuberance of the civil-rights movements that a revival of these songs became apparent once again, some of these appearing with a few words adjusted to suit the occasion. While many of the elders in the marches and meetings were totally aware of their significance and derivation, there were also scores of young people, deprived of this cultural heritage by omission, who thought them to be new songs created by and for the civil-rights movement. It is true that some were created to accompany this crusade, but the majority of these songs were a recapitulation of times past.

However, these examples are but a few of the works available for performance, should one be interested in pursuing them with diligence. One situation is clear in viewing extended choral works by black composers: the "other side of black music" has firm roots and is here to stay. The National Association of Negro Musicians, Inc., a nonprofit group founded in 1919, is dedicated to making this music better known and understood, and such information is available from this group of professionals.

Many other Afro-American composers since the renaissance continue to concentrate on a larger vocal extension of what was once a simple religious expression called the *spiritual*. Composer Ulysses Kay set his pen to a libretto based on Margaret Walker's best-selling book, *Jubilee*, and this opera was designated a Bicentennial event.

6

The Music of American Indians

Charlotte J. Frisbie

The music of American Indians now living is both like and unlike that prevalent at the time of the European colonists' arrival. To understand the styles, meanings, usages, functions, histories, and changes in American Indian music is a life-long endeavor, if you accept the notion that musical sound is only comprehensible when considered within its associated cultural context. It is important to try to understand these similarities and differences, especially when attempting to evaluate the music of the first Americans, its effects on the dominant white culture, and the ways in which it has been affected by the Indians' population reduction by disease, warfare, incarceration, and all the other atrocities that fall on a minority group. And they are still largely confined to reservations, finding the Bicentennial celebration no cause for joy.

Indian music has been relatively undisturbed by the influx of other kinds of music into North America. Similarities with traditional music in the East Asian homeland of the Indians, especially in Siberia, are still discernible, illustrating some of the basic musical preferences of these Mongolians before their migration across the Bering Strait onto this continent, tens of thousands of years ago.[1] Records of explorers, travelers, military personnel, and others in the forefront of the white man's invasion of Indian lands all tell us that music played a major part in the lives of these original inhabitants of our continent. But many of its roles, sounds, instruments, and occasions differed greatly from their equivalents in Western European musical culture.

Perhaps the most striking difference was that the Indian's music was profoundly integrated with daily events. Although the complexity of musical cultures varied (with Eastern, Pueblo, and Northwest Coast groups being the most complex),and although musical styles differed geographically, many groups had numerous songs for use with certain activities. There were songs for protection against the dangers of travel and battle, to invoke assistance of deities during hunting and fishing, to protect crops, to locate lost children and objects, to amuse and quiet children, and to accompany the work of preparing food. There were songs for playing games, telling stories, gambling, social dancing, and feasting.

Much of the music was religious in nature and purpose. Some tribes developed major song cycles to accompany various ceremonies,many of them re-creating mythological heroes and events while transmitting cultural values and their meanings. Music, especially vocal song, was central to many celebrations of life-crisis events, such as naming, puberty, weddings, and funerals, and also in curing rituals, wherein it was often integrated with dancing and the theatrical effects of costuming, mimicry, pantomine, ventriloquism, and other dramatic arts. The proper songs were believed to elicit help from deities, to attract the presence of appropriate spirits and powers, and to help restore the sick to health and harmony.

In most places on the continent, the Europeans found daily music cultures, not dependent on formal settings, trained performers, and rehearsals, plus respectful, reserved, and quiet audiences. Although males often predominated, all who wanted to sing could. There were no professional musicians among the Native Americans. There were some specific songs for men and women, and there were some that could only be used by those with the appropriate sacred knowledge. But in all the Indian cultures the ability to make music and the satisfaction of so doing were commonly shared.

The sounds of this music were as strange to the Europeans as was the degree to which much was integrated into Indian daily life. Melodies were based on collections of tones quite unlike music of the Western scale. Some groups used only a few tones, others employed more; but the tones themselves were not fixed to a standard pitch. The principles and processes of American Indian music were different than in Western Europe; music was transmitted orally from one generation to the next, and no notation system was used. Likewise, there is no evidence of any elaborate theories of scales or composition. Thus, in transcriptions of American Indian melodies it must be understood, as George Herzog has indicated,[2] that "a 'note' does not stand for an objective unit, an ideally constant tone, but for a functional unit, a mere average value around which the variations cluster."

Harmonically the sounds of American Indians were also alien, for while there was a limited amount of part singing in a few places, most music was solely melodic, being sung in unison or with doubling at the octave. In general, the emphasis was on melody rather than harmony, polyphony, or other similar entities.

Rhythmically and structurally, the colonists had fewer surprises, except perhaps for the complexity that some tribal patterns displayed. Flexibility, syncopation, and irregular meters were frequent, and were not easily conveyed by attempts to notate what was heard, using European staff and time signatures. Songs varied in length, contour, and internal organization; some groups preferred relatively large intervals, wide ranges, and descending contours, and many favored repetitions of melodic phrases, with slight alterations during repeats. In general, the tunes varied structurally with tribes and occasions.

Vocal techniques were also available, but basically unfamiliar to many settlers' ears, since many Native Americans favored vocal pulsations, falsettos, nasality, and other techniques that produced sounds which appeared strained and tense to European listeners. The combination of these techniques with the melodic and harmonic aspects of American Indian songs caused many listeners to find the music high and piercing, low and grumbling, or unpleasantly comparable to animal cries.

The music of the American Indians also differed from that of the Europeans in type, since it was predominantly to be sung by individuals or groups of either the same or mixed sex. Instruments did exist, but the paucity of them in North America was obvious. Most common were flutes (both the transverse flute and recorder type), whistles, drums, and rattles, with the latter two being used for accompaniment purposes. Except for some love songs played on flutes by men, it was rare to hear music that was solely instrumental. Instead, the instruments were used to accompany singing, with wind instruments providing rhythmic patterns that either duplicated these in the melody or the dance, or added still another level of complexity.

Textually, the music was also incompatible with Western music both because of the use of Native American languages, such as Kiowa, Kwakiutl, Keresan, and Iroquois, and the use of *vocables* or abstract syllables. The latter sometimes comprised entire texts, and while similar to "tra la la" in some instances, were linguistically unfathomable to the Europeans. Then, too, when song texts could be translated, Europeans did not discover familiar concepts of poetic verse, rhyme, and meter. Instead, they were met with prose texts, wherein ideas might be briefly stated and then given numerous repeats, or given more lengthy, elaborate statements, such as in the following, for the Navajo girl's puberty ceremony:

> *heye neye yaŋa*
> Now she is dressing up her child,
> Now she is dressing up her child,
> Now she is dressing up her child, *holaghei.*
> Now the child of White Shell Woman, now she is dressing her up,
> In the center of the White Shell house, now she is dressing her up,
> On the even white shell floor covering, now she is dressing her up,
> On the smooth floor covering of soft fabrics, now she is dressing her up,
> White Shell Girl, now she is dressing her up,
> Her white shell shoes, now she is dressing her up,
> Her white shell leggings, now she is dressing her up,
> Her white shell clothes, now she is dressing her up,

Now, a perfect white shell having been placed on her forehead,
    now she is dressing her up,
Her white shell head plume, now she is dressing her up,
Now at its tip there are small blue male birds, truly beautiful;
    it is shining at its tip, now she is dressing her up,
They call as they are playing; their voices are beautiful;
    now she is dressing her up,
She is decorated with soft fabrics, now, now she is dressing
    her up,
She is decorated with jewels, now she is dressing her up,
Before her, it is blessed; now she is dressing her up,
Behind her, it is blessed; now she is dressing her up,
Now with long life and everlasting beauty, now she is dressing
    her up,
Now she is dressing up her child,
Now she is dressing up her child, it is said.[3]

Other differences that might be termed *attitudinal* were
obvious between American Indian music and Western European
music. While some Indian groups did have individuals recognized
as composers, in many, songs were contributed by people who
received them from the spirits, through dreams and visions,
during fasting, during illness, and at other times. In still other
groups, songs were viewed as existing since the time of creation.
In some places songs were regarded as individual property, to
be learned by others only after proper arrangements had been
made with the owner. Such knowledge was sacred, and these
songs were equated with other incorporeal property, such as
personal names, pottery designs, curing skills, and divination
talents. Elsewhere, the exchange of songs within and outside the
tribe had no such ownership restrictions. Another difference
was in the attitude toward the need for rehearsal; Pueblo and
Northwest Coast Indians were much concerned about correct
group performances in which certain types of songs were exe-
cuted without error, so they therefore rehearsed them. Many
other groups, however, did not consider practice necessary.

Generations of white settlers reacted ethnocentrically to
Indian music, rejecting the sounds as uncivilized grunts made by
untutored savages, the melodies as barbaric, the tonal systems
as incomplete, and the general effect underdeveloped and not
at all comparable to Western European standards for "music."

A few, however, became excited by what they heard. In one such group were composers and harmonizers such as John Fillmore, Carlos Troyer, Thomas Hastings, and James Murray, who became interested in collecting and notating Indian songs, or, using notations of others, to set the songs to Western European harmonies and render them palatable for performance in concert halls with piano accompaniment. Other composers found fresh challenges in the melodic ideas, tonal systems, intervallic preferences, and rhythmic patterns in Indian songs; they borrowed these elements, using them as actual and inspirational bases for new compositions of their own. Witness for example, the second orchestral suite, *Indian Suite*, and the selection, "Indian Lodge" in *Woodland Sketches* by Edward MacDowell, as well as some of the works of Arthur Farwell, Harvey Loomis, Charles Wakefield Cadman, Charles S. Skilton, Charles Griffes, Thurlon Lieurance, and Frederic Jacobi. These compositions in some cases enlivened interest in the music of Native Americans, and regretfully in others established stereotypes that have been perpetuated right into our own generation.

With the advent of the Edison phonograph and its successful use in field recordings of Passamaquoddy Indian music in Maine by ethnologist Jesse Walter Fewkes in 1890, a new era began. Such music, when performed in settings open to outsiders, could be recorded, preserved, collected, and studied. Among the earliest collectors of American Indian music were Fewkes, Alice Fletcher, Frances Densmore, Natalie Curtis (Burlin), and Washington Matthews. Some of their collections were used by music teachers as data bases to support arguments about the existence of scales and harmonic melody in American Indian music, but, in general, in the late nineteenth and early twentieth centuries, preservation was enough.

The twentieth century brought an expansion of interest on the part of some musicians to include the music of non-Western peoples in their studies. From these beginnings, comparative musicological studies were started, and interests established that led in 1955 to the founding of the Society for Ethnomusicology, which now has over 1,900 members. Within the discipline of ethnomusicology, which represents a combination of music and anthropology, are many specialists in American Indian music, its technical aspects, stylistic varieties, performance techniques, development trends, and relation to Indian cultures.

Thanks to the work of ethnomusicologists (see Notes and Other References for some of the outstanding research), we have learned a great deal about American Indian music. Vocal styles, melodic contours, rhythmic patterns, and other features have been mapped and shown to cluster geographically into music areas.[4] Studies have been made of specific musical cultures and genres. Numerous other specialized reports are available on such topics as the process of composition, construction of particular instruments, and acculturation in musical styles. These labors have served to disseminate information to the scientific and lay communities; to involve more people, institutions, and archives in field collecting and research; and to identify problems for future research. Another result has been to encourage Indians themselves to become reinvolved in their own musical traditions, through visiting-artist programs, lecture-demonstration tours, enrollment in academic degree programs, and publishing. All these increase familiarity with the American Indian musical idiom.

An Indian composer, Louis Ballard, has become established and prolific, and, through his efforts at the Institute for American Indian Arts in Santa Fe, has made the transmission of Indian musical cultures part of youth education. Other schools have instituted American Indian singing groups, many of which include representatives of ten to twenty tribes who travel, performing a variety of musical events from their own and other tribes' heritages.

The exposure of today's Americans to Indian music is thus many sided. Movies, television, and radio shows feature American Indian music backgrounds, some of them authentic. Powwows are regularly held in many big cities with public attendance. School groups, individuals, and small tribal groups have entered the recording market, producing albums and tapes; some are samplers in nature and others are devoted to a specific genre. These recordings are marketed under such labels as Indian House, American Indian Soundchief, and Canyon Records, and are readily available. Then there are the special concerts and programs sponsored by archives, museums, scientific societies, academic institutions, and individuals and groups of artists on tour. Introduction to American Indian music is also infiltrating primary and secondary education as music educators become increasingly interested in introducing world cultures to their students. The opportunities for exposure to American Indian music, or rather to selected aspects of it, have increased greatly as have our abilities to understand varieties of music in their cultural contexts.

However, it is important to remember that acculturation is not a one-way street. While music is usually cited as one of the most persistent elements in culture, American Indian music itself, both in general and in specific tribal musical styles and genres, has been changing. The music has not existed in a vacuum nor remained totally unaffected by generations of contact with settlers, despite the basic incompatibility of Indian music with that of Western Europe. There are few, if any, Indians left who have never seen a white person, heard a radio, or looked at a newspaper; many reservations are also within the reach of television. An expanding number of Indians are moving to cities in search of better living conditions. Migratory work, military service, university education, and employment in the economic mainstream all are involved in the modern Indian experience, and Indian music cannot help but show the effects.

As Nettl has established,[5] contacts with European settlers both enriched and impoverished American Indian musical cultures. Some of the changes are obvious. Through the efforts of Christian missionaries and early schoolteachers, Native Americans were introduced to Christian hymns and thus to the associated Western concepts of part singing, melodic lines, scales, and harmonies. It is possible that the introduction of such genres inhibited the nascent development of native polyphony[6]; in any case, in many mission church services today, standard hymn tunes are sung with texts translated and sung in the native language of the converts. Mass media have brought familiarity with other genres, such as rock-and-roll or country-and-western performing bands, as well as individual big-name artists.

Other developments that stem from contact and are more native in orientation include the increasing attraction to the Native American Church that has recently led to the spread of Peyote music, just as did the earlier Ghost Dance movement with its associated musical styles. The trend toward pan-Indianism, the reemphasis on being Indian, and the reawakening of interests in tribal identities and heritages have also had effects on music. Indians are now in more frequent contact with each other, across tribal lines, and have especially become well

aware of each other's secular genre and songs. This has led to
the dominance of the Plains style of music at fairs, festivals, and
powwows, since much of the pan-Indianism is based on Plains
cultural patterns adopted nationally as symbols of Indianness.
Thus, as is true with the music of other minority groups, that
of the American Indians today speaks for group heritage and
identity.[7]

But contact also has contributed to some musical depletion.
As new song and dance genres are introduced and transmitted,
others decline. This is particularly true in the religious area,
where individuals and groups knowledgeable of song cycles,
sets of dream songs, and the like are declining in number, and
fewer songs are being composed. Some of the rituals have become
defunct; others have been abbreviated to adapt them to weekend
performances when laborers are free to attend, or to public
occasions, where Indians are outnumbered in the audiences.
Some of these alterations have led to the disappearance of
entire sets of songs or to their abbreviation, so that only one in
a series is performed. Individual songs are also being shortened.

These changes have led to a preference for those genres
that can be performed at tribal fairs, powwows, and on records
and tape. The social dance songs are coming to the foreground,
whereas in the past they constituted only a small part of the
total musical heritage. It is important to realize that recorded
examples of American Indian music are not all there is to these
musical traditions, and that the very act of recording is in itself
helping to undercut extant repertoires.

Variety and complexity are further reduced by changes in
song texts. While much singing is still done in tribal languages,
there is an increased use of vocables rather than native words
in entire song texts. Such changes make possible public render-
ings of songs formerly restricted to sacred usage, and facilitate
the transmission and sharing of songs on the national, pan-
Indian level. An increased use of English words in song texts,
particularly secular, social ones is also noticeable.[8] An example
of one such social dance song that can be heard today on many
reservations throughout the country in different versions is as
one Navajo sang it to me:

Yo-wo-o wo-wo'o, wo-o wo wo'o, wo'o wo weyą heye neye yaŋa
Yo-wo-o wo-wo'o, wo-o wo wo'o, wo'o wo weyą heye neye yaŋa

You might know, you might know
How I love you, *wo wo wo-o wo weyǫ, heye neye yaŋa*
I don't care if you're married
I'll get you yet, *wo wo-o wo weyǫ, heye neye yaŋa*
Yo-wo-o wo-wo'o, wo-o wo wo'o, wo-o wo weyǫ heye neye yaŋa
Yo-wo-o wo-wo'o, wo-o wo wo'o, wo-o wo weyǫ heye neye yǫ

Other changes, primarily attitudinal, accompany the simultaneous enrichment and impoverishment of repertoires. There is increasing recognition of the human derivation of compositions, and a new emphasis on the importance of knowing many songs and how to perform them before audiences. Enter the professional musician and the whole concept of music as professional entertainment business, with its emphasis on rehearsals, staging, tour management, industry production, and weekly ratings! Concomitantly one finds more subtle changes, especially in the area of intonation, with the variant intervals closest to the Western-tempered scale given preference by Indians who sing to the accompaniment of or perform music on such instruments as amplified guitars and electric pianos.

The American Indian musical heritage now available to other Americans is, therefore, obviously mixed. It includes access to many aspects of traditional Native American music (through collections, archives, scholarly studies, and reservation performances open to the public), as well as to an increasingly secular idiom. In both the traditional and contemporary music, the effects of acculturation are obvious in the song genres, vocal styles, performance settings, techniques, language, and instrumentation. American Indian music has drastically changed in its use and function, yet it continues to be rich, varied, unique, and viable. No matter what your preference is—the unique Navajo yeibichai falsetto sound, the ribald texts of Eskimo song-duel compositions, the composition ideas of modern Indian composers, or the Indian elements in the latest album by a Plains rock-and-roll group—there are rewards in the heritage for every attentive listener.

Notes

1. Bruno Nettl, *Folk and Traditional Music of the Western Continents*, Second edition (Englewood Cliffs, N.J.: Prentice-Hall, 1973), p. 158.

2. George Herzog, "A Comparison of Pueblo and Pima Musical Styles," *Journal of American Folklore* 49 (1936): 286-87.

3. Charlotte J. Frisbie, *Kinaaldá: A Study of the Navaho Girl's Puberty Ceremony* (Middletown, Conn.: Wesleyan University, Press, 1967), pp. 296-97.

4. Bruno Nettl, "North American Indian Musical Styles," *Memoirs of the American Folklore Society*, no. 45 (1954); Bruno Nettl, "Musical Areas Reconsidered: A Critique of North American Indian Research," in *Essays in Musicology in Honor of Dragan Plamenac on His 70th Birthday* (Pittsburgh: University of Pittsburgh Press, 1969), pp. 181-89.

5. Bruno Nettl, "The Western Impact on World Music: Africa and the American Indians," in *Contemporary Music and Music Cultures*, eds. Charles Hamm, Bruno Nettl, and Ronald Byrnside (Englewood Cliffs, N.J.: Prentice-Hall, 1975), pp. 101-124.

6. Ibid., p. 115.

7. Ibid., pp. 121-22.

8. Willard Rhodes, "North American Indian Music in Transition," *International Folk Music Council Journal* 15 (1963): 9-14.

Other References

Crawford, David. "The Jesuit Relations and Allied Documents, Early Sources for an Ethnography of Music among American Indians." *Ethnomusicology* 11, no. 2 (1967): 199-206.

Kurath, Gertrude (with Garcia, Antonio). "Music and Dance of the Tewa Pueblos." *Museum of New Mexico Research Records*, no. 8. Santa Fe, N.M.: Museum of New Mexico Press, 1970.

McAllester, David. "Peyote Music." *Viking Fund Publications in Anthropology*, no. 13. New York: Viking Fund, 1949.

Merriam, Alan. "Ethnomusicology of the Flathead Indians." *Viking Fund Publications in Anthropology*, no. 44. New York: Viking Fund, 1967.

Nettl, Bruno. "Studies in Blackfoot Indian Musical Culture." *Ethnomusicology* 11, no. 2:141-60; 11, no. 3:293-309; 12, no. 1:11-48; 12, no. 2:192-207.

Roberts, Helen. "Musical Areas in Aboriginal North America." *Yale University Publications in Anthropology*, no. 12. New Haven, Conn.: Yale University Press, 1936.

Stevenson, Robert. "Written Sources for Indian Music until 1882." *Ethnomusicology* 17, no. 1 (1973a): 1-40.

_____. "English Sources for Indian Music until 1882." *Ethnomusicology* 17, no. 3 (1973b): 399-442.

7

American Folksong: Some Comments on the History of Its Collection and Archiving*

Joseph C. Hickerson

Folk music and song are the musical/poetic aspects of folklore. Folklore has four major characteristics, and definitions of folklore usually involve at least two, sometimes three, and sometimes all four of the qualities following:

1) Folklore exists through time, and we often use the word *tradition* in connection with it.

2) Folklore is *transmitted orally* or by example from person to person, thence from community to community and from one period of time to another. These elements of tradition and oral transmission often lead to the definition of verbal folklore as *oral tradition*. They also yield an important and necessary corollary, namely, the characteristic *variation* exhibited by folklore forms.

---

*This chapter refers specifically to the history and collection of the Library of Congress Archive of Folk Song, of which Mr. Hickerson is the archivist. It is taken from transcriptions of workshop lectures by Mr. Hickerson, then edited for this volume.

3) Folklore exists not only through the actions and utterances of individual persons, but also within collective bodies of people frequently referred to as *folk groups*. Folk groups are those people who share traditions passed on orally or by example. They are generally isolated, homogeneous, and cohesive, at least to some extent. The relative isolation may be through geographic, economic, ethnic, religious, or familial delimitations, or factors of age, social group, occupation, and so forth.

4) Folklore lives in *events*—in the singing of a song, the making of music, or the telling of a story—within a *small group*, such as a family circle, or a gathering at a pub, at work, at school, at church, "behind the barn"—there is where folklore really lives.

The history of "collecting" or documenting the materials of folklore goes back perhaps 250 years in Europe, and about 150 years in this country. Certain people became interested in traditional songs and tales, and began collecting folklore as well as they could with the meager collecting resources at their disposal. In the early days, the only methods of collecting were either to find the material already written out, or to write it down in the presence of the singer, storyteller, or other "informant." Such methods were adequate for garnering the bare bones of text and tune, but fell short of documenting folklore accurately and contextually. A collector interested in a song but unable to keep up with the performer would have to interrupt, probably several times, with, "Wait a minute. . ., please start again. . ., not so fast. . ., what was that again?. . .," and so on, and would get a rendition of the song that was not totally realistic.

So it is easy to imagine the jubilation and excitement of a hundred years ago at the news that Thomas Alva Edison had invented a device for recording sound. This device was initially a very cumbersome machine that recorded on a wax cylinder, but it proved useful and valuable in early fieldwork.

The first documentation in sound of any sort of oral tradition anywhere in the world was by a young anthropologist at Harvard University's Peabody Museum, Jesse Walter Fewkes, in March 1890. Fewkes learned of Edison's device and thought that it might be a useful tool to take along to the Southwest, where he was working in anthropology and archaeology, to record songs, tales, and similar events. But he wanted to try it out first, so he took it to Calais, Maine, to record some members of the Passamaquoddy Indian tribe. For years after Fewkes's death, these historic cylinders were considered "missing," and scholars supposed they were lost forever. About six years ago Professor David P. McAllester, while searching for some other cylinders in the back rooms of the Peabody Museum, found some old wax recordings covered with dust—the Fewkes cylinders. Soon afterward, these recordings were acquired by the Library of Congress in exchange for a set of tape copies. Our chief sound engineer, Robert B. Carneal, did the copying, and now we can hear these first folklore recordings in all their scratchy glory. In one of them we hear Dr. Fewkes announcing where he is and the date—18 March 1890. Then we heard the sixty-year-old Indian, Noel Joseph, speaking in Passamaquoddy and describing what he is about to sing. Then comes the song, that is unusually clear for a recording of this age. On another cylinder, Fewkes—obviously enjoying this novel scientific device—is talking into the machine himself, saying, "Good morning, Mr. Phonograph," and "Thank you for letting us come and record your songs and stories."

Back from his trip, Dr. Fewkes enthusiastically admonished his fellow anthropologists and folklorists to get this machine, and to record the music, songs, tales, and language of the people they were collecting from. He stressed that with these wax cylinders researchers could gain a form of scientific documentation virtually equal to the "specimens" of the natural sciences.

The anthropologists of this country paid heed to Fewkes, but the folklorists did not. In the 1890s perhaps two dozen anthropologists began using these machines. In the first decade of this century, many more did—a lot of them students of anthropology at Columbia University under Franz Boas.

In 1908 the federal government began sponsoring the recording of oral traditions, when the Smithsonian's Bureau of American Ethnology (B.A.E.) sent Frances Densmore to record Indian material. She began with the Chippewa (Ojibway) Indians in her native Minnesota. During the next 25 years, she made approximately 2,600 cylinders among a large variety of Indian groups. Over 1,000 others were also acquired by the BAE. These cylinders eventually entered the Library of Congress collections. The Library copied the Densmore cylinders in the late 1940s, and has since issued seven long-playing records from the collection.

The transition from cylinder to disc recordings, and also from acoustic to electronic equipment, occurred in the late 1920s and early 1930s. With both steps the sound quality improved, and fieldworkers were able to record for longer periods of time at a sitting—instead of a two-minute cylinder, a four-minute disc; and by the 1940s, eight and fifteen minutes to a side. Disc recordings were made through the 1940s, when they were succeeded briefly by wire and then permanently by tape.

With whatever equipment they used, the scientists of folklore and anthropology have been concerned primarily with the material they were working to preserve, and—as professional recording engineers have been quick to mention—less so with the efficient operation of equipment. One anthropologist in New York State, William Fenton, who recorded with discs in the 1940s on the reservations of the Iroquois tribes, used the Indians themselves as recording engineers. They had their own radio stations, and the brother of one of the chief singers actually operated the equipment.

Almost always the early collectors of Indian folklore—and this is still a strong tendency—looked for the oldest songs and the oldest singers to exemplify the most ancient examples of tradition. As a result there has always been the mood of desperation among collectors to speed the collecting process, because the singers and the songs were in danger of dying out. It was not until the 1940s that collectors began to pay serious attention to the newer songs of the younger Indians. One of these researchers was Professor Willard Rhodes, an ethnomusicologist at Columbia University, who spent several summers in the Northwest and Southwest for the Bureau of Indian Affairs, Department of the Interior, recording with equipment provided partly by the Library of Congress. From the start, in 1941, he was strongly interested in current musical forms in addition to the centuries-old genres, recording songs with English-language words, Christian hymns in native languages, and the like.

Most of the anthropologists in the first twenty or thirty years of that discipline, starting in the 1880s, came from the natural sciences. It was always part of their work to go out into the field, and the use of paraphernalia came naturally to them. In 1890, when Jesse Walter Fewkes urged his fellows, including the folklorists, to take to the field with recording devices, the collectors of English ballads, cowboy songs, and Negro spirituals were generally at universities in English or other humanistic departments, and they were primarily library scholars. These humanistic folklorists abjured equipment. It was not until after World War I, about 1921, that collectors of folklore went in systematic search for their basic materials with recording machines.

The prime interest of the early folklorists in this country, even though they did not record it until much later, was the ballad—the narrative folksong such as the ones that came over from England and Scotland. One of the pioneers in ballad recording was Sidney Robertson Cowell, who went into the field in the 1930s for several government agencies and, with a disc machine, recorded an old man at Boyd's Cove, North Carolina, singing in one of the oldest styles—a style that collectors had rarely found in England. Folklorists made many such discoveries of archaic language and singing styles, all but extinct in the British Isles but still preserved in remote regions of the United States. One of the characteristics of the old style is the repeated line, and anyone attempting to transcribe that music would have a difficult time bringing it into any regular meter and still maintain the integrity of the piece. The earlier collectors with pencil and paper tended to ignore these important stylistic variations; the sound recordings helped to raise the importance of these nuances to student and musician alike.

Like the collectors of Indian music, the early ballad and folksong collectors paid most of their attention to the older music of older persons until the 1940s. They also appreciated that folk music is just one aspect of the verbal expression of a culture. At the same time as the early study of ballads, some of the same scholars became interested in old narratives that came to this country from Europe and Africa. But it was not until the 1930s and 1940s that they began to record these storytellers on acetate discs, eventually with about fifteen minutes on a side, and were able to make recordings of these longer forms under studio conditions.

One notable collector of folksongs in the country, Cecil J. Sharp, was an Englishman who at the age of forty started collecting traditional dance and song in his homeland. After some fifteen years of collecting he came to the United States on a speaking tour. He met someone who was connected with a school in North Carolina who said that some of the people in her neighborhood sang the same songs as the ones he had collected in England. Sharp was immediately interested, and arranged three collecting expeditions around 1916-18 in North Carolina and Kentucky, accompanied by a young lady named Maude Karpeles, who in November 1975 celebrated her ninetieth birthday.

Sharp used no recording machine. Back in England he had tried it and found it too cumbersome. He said the singers did not like the apparatus and that it was not necessary for him to use it. His practice was simply to jot down the tune as the song was sung, while Ms. Karpeles noted the text in shorthand. We have a great corpus of songs and ballads that they collected in this country, primarily from British and Scottish sources. Since they did not make recordings, it has not been possible to verify their transcriptions; we simply have to trust their manuscript notations.

One trend in this country has been a developing interest not in transplanted materials but in native American folksongs. Among the first to collect these was a Texan, John Avery Lomax. At Harvard University he studied under George Lyman Kittredge, an early folklore scholar, who urged Lomax to collect some of the cowboy songs and other material from his home state. Except for perhaps a couple of dozen cylinders made before World War I, he did all his collecting in the old-fashioned handwritten way. In fact, many of his texts were given to him by other people.

Lomax was also one of those early folklorists who "collected" the songs by learning them. Since many of the original singers died before anyone could record them, some of the songs that Lomax collected lived on only in his memory or in the recollections of his family, as extrapolated and interpreted by their own set of musical preferences, conscious or unconscious.

When many people in this country think of anything in connection with the folk music collections of the Library of Congress, they associate it with the Lomax name. We still get letters addressed to John A. Lomax, who died in 1948, and to Alan Lomax, his son, who last was employed by the Library in 1942. But they did not establish the Archive of Folk Song, nor have they been actively involved in its direction for the last thirty-five years.

What was originally called the Archive of American Folk Song was established in 1928, through the efforts of folklorist

Robert Winslow Gordon and the then Chief of the Library's
Music Division, Carl Engel, who, like a good many of his musicological colleagues in this country and Europe, had some interest
in indigenous music. As early as 1906, composers such as Percy
Grainger and Béla Bartók recorded folksongs to get accurate
documentation of musical materials as sources for their compositions. Carl Engel had some idea of the importance of this kind
of documentation, and he persuaded a number of individuals to
donate money to start a national folksong archive.

Robert W. Gordon, who became the first director of the
Archive, had studied at Harvard, taught at Berkeley, and was one
of the two folklorists in this country to begin to record Anglo- and
Afro-American folksongs with a cylinder machine. (The other
was Frank C. Brown of Duke University, who concentrated on
North Carolina folklore.) Gordon collected in California with the
cylinder machine as early as 1920. He had what he called a
"field station" in Darien, Georgia, and also spent some time
recording around Asheville, North Carolina. By the time he came
to the Library of Congress in 1928, he had around 550 cylinders
and thousands of songs in manuscript form. While at the Library,
Gordon experimented with portable disc equipment, and in 1932
he made a pioneering field trip to Virginia, West Virginia, and
Kentucky with a disc machine.

Aside from recording, Gordon had another fruitful avenue
for garnering song materials; it had been used by others but
never as effectively. From 1923 to 1928, Gordon had a column
in a monthly magazine called *Adventure* entitled "Old Songs
That Men Have Sung." Through these columns and the corres-
pondence they generated, he received nearly 4,000 letters containing more than 10,000 song items.

Unfortunately, the Archive's private money had dwindled
by 1932, and it no longer could offer any salary for a director.
Early the next year, John A. Lomax came to Washington. He
had recently renewed his interest in folksong collecting, and
came to the Library with a specific project in mind: to record
the work songs of black inmates in Texas prisons. Here, Lomax
felt, was a "classic" example of a folk group, with forced isolation
and homogeneity, and active song creation. He received equipment and blank discs from the Library in 1933, and thereby
began an association with the Library of Congress that lasted

until his death in 1948. He was originally listed as Curator of the Archive (a kind of dollar-a-year job), and later as Honorary Curator and Consultant.

In 1937 Congress finally appropriated money for one position in the Archive, an assistant-in-charge, and that job was held until 1942 by the most active of John Lomax's progeny in the realm of folk collecting—Alan Lomax.

Starting around 1935 some other federal agencies formed under the New Deal began actively collecting folklore and folk music. In every case they began their operations and often continued them with direct assistance from the Library of Congress Archive of Folk Song. For example, the Resettlement Administration, which later became the Farm Security Administration, had a Special Skills Division under the direction of Charles Seeger, which sent out several people with disc machines obtained from the Library of Congress.

The Federal Writers' Project, under the Work Projects (formerly Work Progress) Administration (W.P.A.), collected folklore and allied material in virtually every state, though largely without the aid of sound recordings. The direction of the WPA projects was provided first by John A. Lomax and then by B. A. Botkin. In some localities these projects did use machines, usually obtained from the Library of Congress.

By this time the cities had been discovered as sources of folklore. Urban areas can have just as many traditions that exhibit the criteria of folklore as the isolated valleys and byways of the more romantically ideal folklore regions, such as the Ozarks, the deep South, and Appalachia. One fascinating example of city folklore was collected in 1939 by Herbert Halpert and David Hatch for the WPA's Federal Theater Project. A black street vendor calling himself "Fish Man" made up the following verse on the spot: "Now I'm makin' records for the WPA / Now when you hear 'em don't you swing and sway / Don't you fuss, don't you fight, don't be right / 'Cause those records gonna play all night.''

As sound recording equipment evolved in sophistication, and as it became more accessible to folklore collectors, it not only improved the fidelity of the recorded material but also increased the continuous recording time available for a single piece. From the early two-minute cylinder it advanced to four minutes on the Dictaphone cylinder and early discs; in the late

1930s, the 33⅓-rpm speed became available, allowing about eight minutes on a side, and then in the 1940s on professional disc equipment using 16-inch acetate discs, one could record at least fifteen minutes without interruption.

Some collectors found ways of surmounting the time limitation to record even longer forms. For example, John Henry Faulk collected Texas Negro church services in the early 1940s on two disc machines. He would start with the A side on the first machine, and when it was about to run out he would begin the A side of the second machine. Next he would pick up with the B sides of the first and then the second machine, so it is possible now, by splicing together a tape copy, to get a continuous church service of more than an hour's duration.

With the improvements in equipment, and the increase in people and institutions interested in studying this material, folklore recordings began to improve in substance and quality. At first collectors were so desperate to get just what they wanted within short durations of recorded time that they often would have the singer sing only one or two verses, and get the rest of the text by hand. It took a while for collectors to realize that the most untypical verses in terms of melodic content are likely to be the initial ones.

Recording techniques began approaching their present flexibility in the late 1940s with the brief use of magnetic wire and its more permanent cousin, magnetic tape. Recording also became less expensive. As each new medium came along, however, it began with the recording of short, fragmented, truncated pieces of recorded information, developing later to more extended recordings. It was a considerable gain when a collector could sit down with someone and record conversation, stories, songs, and ballads all in one session, with a minimum of self-consciousness as the informant got accustomed to the experience. In the 1940s, for example, John Lomax was able to return with improved disc equipment to some of the cowboys that he had collected from earlier, with and without recordings, this time making extended interviews that contained contextual information on the singers and the songs, in addition to the songs themselves.

The first tape recordings of folk music in this country were made in 1947, and tape equipment became widely available by the early fifties. When you listen to some of the old tapes (great care is necessary because the first tape materials were

much inferior to what we have now, and they may fall apart),
you find that they were being operated like the old cylinder
machines or early discs. Only when the singer was ready to
begin would the collector turn on the recorder, sometimes a
little behind the singer. I don't know how many taped renditions
of songs start with the third word of the first verse, and end as
soon as the song is over, virtually before the last note has faded.

As people got more comfortable with the equipment, and
the tape became more accessible, folklorists began recording
more than just the isolated song or story. They developed what
has been called the "vacuum-cleaner method." The tape recorder
would be set up, turned on, and left to run. This made possible
the combination of interview and singing. If there was more than
one informant in the room, the collector could get some interaction, and ideas of how people think and behave about their
music, in addition to the isolated bits and pieces of song. This
has become very important in certain areas of folklore studies,
which analyze the events, the contexts, and the attitudes of
folklore performers and performances.

Collectors who set out to record only certain kinds of folksong or music may find that they are missing important material
if they reject other things—and they may be hurting their chances
of getting anything. If they are looking for only one kind of song,
and the informant starts to do something else that he likes, only
to be interrupted with, "No, I don't want that," then the person
being recorded is likely to be "turned off." It is gratifying that
more and more collectors are becoming interested in total repertory, and not only of song material but also stories, local
legends, comments, and interplay that can be as fascinating as
the main subject of the recording.

As the study of folklore and folk music has progressed, the
Library of Congress Archive of Folk Song has expanded its
notion of what it should cover. Starting with an interest in American folk music, our national repository of documentary raw
materials (manuscripts and recordings) of folk music has expanded to include all aspects of folklore, and also a good representation of international folk music. Physically, the Archive
occupies two rooms in the northeast corner of the main building
of the Library of Congress. Our Reading/Listening Room is open
to the public from 8:30 to 5:00 weekdays (except holidays), and
contains over 3,000 books and other materials for reference.

Our own series of recorded folk music and lore has been issued under the Library of Congress label since 1942. There are now sixty-six recordings in the regular series, and another fifteen recently issued as part of the Bicentennial.

A set of these records is available for listening by visitors without prior appointment; any other listening can be arranged by appointment. Tape copies of unissued recordings can often be ordered for a special duplication fee.

One of our services has been to compile bibliographies, and at present we have 125 of these special subject lists and directories available for distribution. Currently, the Archive has a staff of two—myself and a librarian. There is also a secretary who is paid out of special funds. A lot of our work has been done with private support, and recently with the aid of a series of student volunteer interns, some of whom receive credit from their schools for their work with us. Further details on the Archive's operations, services, recordings, and bibliographies can be obtained on request from our office at the Library of Congress, Washington, D.C. 20540.

8

Popular Music: The Sounds of the Many

K. Peter Etzkorn

One measure of the impact of America on the world is the universal acceptance of its popular music. Wherever one goes, in the communist and socialist nations, in the NATO countries, in the developing centers of Africa, Latin America, and Asia, the sounds of American music greet the traveler. American lyrics are sung without a trace of an accent in far-distant bistros, though the singer may not know any English. Performers of America's popular music travel widely for personal appearances, and in even more dispersed places this music is heard on records. Some of these recordings are made from broadcasts of Western radio stations or programs of the Voice of America, and are distributed from hand to hand. Along with Coca-Cola and blue jeans, American popular music has made its impact on the cultures of this world.

American popular music draws on the rich treasury of cultures brought over from the Old World and Africa. The migrants to America, whether forced or free, brought with them folk melodies and vernacular traditions that sustained them in difficult hours, and helped them to celebrate their becoming part of the new experience. Many of the musical occasions called for

119

religious expressions uniting all and bridging distinctions of rank and social standing so characteristic of Europe of those times.

In the nineteenth century, towns of the original colonies began to develop into metropolitan centers with more stratified social distances between the earlier and the newer Americans. At the same time, what had been trading posts farther west were becoming fast-growing cities. There a new culture of the common man was once again created, not unlike the earlier experiences of the Atlantic coast settlements.

Opportunities in the United States attracted new citizens from places where there was political or economic repression. By 1850 the aborted democratic revolutions in Germany, for example, had brought a major wave of immigrants to the Middlewest and particularly to St. Louis. Students of American music point out that the formerly popular English music was overtaken by the German. Rather than an amalgamated popular music, combining the African, English, French, and German traditions on fairly equal terms, something reminiscent of the Austrian-German Volkslied began to dominate popular music. Hitchcock informs us that Americans rejected the American present as stimulus for subject matter and modeled their concert formats, their musical societies, and their formal musical instruction on European precedents.[1]

It was the publication of sheet music, beginning in the mid-nineteenth century and prepared for the musical amateur, that brought themes from American life into song lyrics. These lyrics dealt with love, changing modes of life, events of the day, and familiar topics of assured interest to the public beginning to be shaped into the more uniform American audience of the next century. The complexity of language and cultural and social traditions evident in the popular music of those days were also reflected in the minstrel shows performed in the "opera houses" of all larger communities, from the Appalachians to Virginia City, Nevada, and other entertainment halls. Various ethnic and religious communities cultivated a more traditional music related to their histories of settlement in America, as evidenced in the cases of the California Missions, the Shakers, and the German settlers in Pennsylvania. Even here what sheet music may not have accomplished in diluting tradition was brought about eventually by radio and television.

Few slaves were permitted to maintain their African communal ways in America and their musical traditions were inhibited and blended with the music of their owners. Yet their basic musicality was not lost, and it became, along with contributions from the Caribbean, truly American popular music.

Hitchcock reports that the Negro spirituals, "which were hardly discussed in print and never transcribed before the Reconstruction period after the Civil War, had their source in the evangelical song of the great revivals in the American South and West in the period after 1800."[2] Little documentation exists for the reconstruction of the musical life of the common man in those days. We may draw some inferences from scant sources, from pictures, and from our knowledge of other communities. We can imagine that there were people who would pick up an instrument and accompany a dance, take part in a dirge, or celebrate the change of season. We do not know what was actually performed, nor what it sounded like. What was to become the indigenous elements of American ragtime and early jazz would be found in this music, with its offbeat accents and improvisations that the American Negro introduced in playing European folk-dance music.[3] Under different circumstances, the traditions, conventions, and performance skills of black Americans would later emerge as statements of a self-conscious ethnic identity. Such cities as Cincinnati and St. Louis began to serve a market of popular musicians through the publishing of sheet music, mainly for piano players of limited technical facility.

The basic pattern of music publishing and distribution, which began to take form at the time of the linkage between the coasts by the transcontinental railroads, was to remain in force until radio broadcasting and recording introduced major modifications. Popular music became established at that time, separate from the philharmonic and choral societies and the church musicians. Popular music became a product of the business world of America to be manufactured, distributed, and sold at a profit to the entrepreneur.

The mass production of upright pianos brought their costs within reach of a large market of average Americans. While earlier days had seen the popularity of instruments like the banjo and the violin, the collection of sheet music in the stacks of the New York Public Library indicates that popular music was mainly arranged for pianists and that publication centered in a few large cities.

Music publishers had in-house arrangers who would write out the score for a song submitted on a lead-sheet (melody with text), or would even prepare the latter, if the composer was not able to notate the melody. Many a well-known tunesmith lacked the skill for notating his popular tunes, among them Irving Berlin. The standard format would be a four-liner with the first line of the melody being repeated once, a second melodic element soon returning the piece to a modified repetition of the first melody. Thus the basic musical format can be summarized as an AABA style. The catchier the melody and the more appealing the theme of the lyric, the more likely was such a tune to please the audience. The publisher's investment in reimbursing the composer and printing and promoting the composition was staked on as wide a distribution as he could arrange. His problem was to find a way to attract public attention.

The song plugger as a fixture of the popular-music business made his entrance. Not only would song pluggers attempt to persuade band leaders or singers to feature their songs over their competitors, but they would also arrange for the tunes to be performed in store sheet-music departments. The publisher's financial return was from the sales of sheet music, and not from performance royalties. Only with the founding of the American Society of Composers and Publishers (A.S.C.A.P.) would royalties begin to be systematically collected and distributed to authors, composers, and publishers.

American popular music gradually took on characteristics that differentiate it from the cultivated and vernacular music of Europe, or the tribal music of Africa. Much popular music reached audiences without musical literacy at informal social gatherings and via musical imitation and oral transmission.

To differentiate American popular music from European examples in musicological terms alone is frequently difficult if at all possible. What, for example, makes the waltz "Meet Me in St. Louis" an example of American popular music and not that of an Austrian waltz? The lyrics make a difference, but there would also need to be considered the audiences, the setting to which the song is addressed, its rather democratic appeal, and its basic simplicity, which crosses ethnic, class, and residential traditions. Hardly any of these differentia, however, would be narrowly "musical." Its music would be enjoyed by the high and the not-so-high, it would be played at social affairs and hummed spontaneously. Its simple arrangements, sold over the counter at dime stores, would be repeated by the sales girls and performed by piano students whose parents would be pleased to hear their child play music that they recognized. Serious composers, such as Charles Ives, would also turn to these melodies to transform them into stunning renditions of symphonic music. Composers employing contemporary popular melodies for larger, complex works tend to have been able to count on success. One is led to think of Beethoven, Mozart, Brahms, Dvorak, and Bartók. Yet Ives is only belatedly coming into his own. To some extent this is related to the preference of American musicians for European composers.

In comparison to the number of people whose tastes and aspirations were shaped by music masters from overseas through instruction in cultivated music, the great majority of the American people was closer to its popular music. Might it not have been the dream of many a youngster (and of his immigrant parents) to see himself on the bandstand playing a solo on the Fourth of July, in front of everybody and for everybody? Here the rules for acclaim were public and shared, and not taken from the cultivated classes of the Old World—a world that some had consciously rejected, and to which others had no cultural connections whatsoever. It is not surprising, then, that the typical American character of our popular music would have to be looked for in the social dimensions that this music created and filled.

Variations of themes and musical content of our popular music have certainly been related to the history of immigration and settlement. Changes in modes of transportation, occupation, industrialization, and rural versus urban styles of living also are reflected. The younger set has traditionally been more connected with the visibility of this music through its employment in the public places of organized dances and courtship. And throughout history the activities of the young have always been observed by the older set. Much critical attention to the rock-and-roll music of the recent past, then, only highlights a recurring feature of popular music.

Time and again the introduction of a new style has been accompanied by critical voices lamenting the passing of the familiar and decrying the new as morally inferior and dangerous. With new styles of popular music frequently providing the foundation of new dances and, hence, impact on physical relations between the sexes on the dance floor, much commentary about music may express disguised sexual anxieties. Indeed many of these aesthetic commentaries, purporting to deal with music, are patently couched in nonmusical terms.

Antagonists and protagonists of rock and roll, for example, treat it as a radical departure from the traditional. It becomes associated with various political, social, and sexual revolutionary developments. Yet as music, rock and roll is rather a simplification of the traditional, though in an extended form, breaking through the mold of the AABA pattern and combining the traditional musical elements with new electronic-sound technology. Besides the use of up-to-date electronic technology for sound generation and amplification, it is mainly the nonmusical setting that may be regarded as novel: the dress of performers, their stage movements and social movements offstage, their social origin, and even their limited degree of "musical" training. Then there are the lyrics of their tunes, which glorify private indulgence, arouse social protest, and describe the fears and glories of the outlaw, the drug addict, or the counterculture. These songs sold to teenagers, listened and danced to by youth, give a different picture of America from that portrayed by the songs of the nineteenth century. Here, too, the student of popular music is reminded that the cultural phenomenon of popular music has ramifications beyond music as music. That there is something new, though the music may be old, carries the meaning of musical change into the world of multimedia. What may be experienced as revolutionary music may be its unconventional manner of presentation, its high level of sound amplification, or its performance in a setting where audience and musicians appear to be under the influence of drugs and carried away by its happening, by its being there, by doing it, by merging into one.

In the large and complex society of contemporary America, where there are regional differences in style of life and discernibly formed ethnic traditions, not all popular music is popular with all groups. Indeed there is a movement of culture from subgroups to the larger society simultaneous with a reverse trend to preserve cultural identity of subgroups. Throughout our history this process has also affected the flow of popular music.

Since this field was connected early with business and marketing, the interaction between subgroups and the larger society in the field of popular music was not always as unimpeded as one might wish.

Commercial interests for years supported specialized musical traditions by producing records for highly specialized markets, while at the same time plugging their regular products in the larger market. One consequence of this practice was that the larger market was saturated with a rather uniform product and not exposed to the popular music of the ethnic minority. Another consequence, however, was that the ethnic music was regenerated. In the case of soul music, for example, it was through this mechanism that, with changes in the radio industry, it began to be heard on many AM and FM stations all over America.

What used to be popular music among a restricted group of people became embraced as popular music by a far wider audience. The race records of former years illustrate this process. The formerly restricted base of distribution was challenged by the wide appreciation of jazz, and by the commercial success of record sales outside the formerly limited marketing areas.

The link of popular music to the world of business is of further significance. When music was brought alive for audiences largely by performances from sheet music, the welfare of popular music was closely intertwined with the rise of music publishing and the mass production of the piano. Music publishing became centralized in a few cities, and New York's Tin Pan Alley took on the dominant role. The music was selected for publication by individuals who lived in similar circumstances and experienced life from offices even in the same building—first on Fourteenth Street and later the Brill Building off Times Square. Songwriters would coax publishers to buy their songs and publishers would, in turn, attempt to coax band leaders to play them. When a successful big-city band would travel around the country, the fashions of the city would be spread, with sales of sheet music reflecting this diffusion process.

The mass production of the phonograph did not greatly affect the New York dominance, though it brought other changes. The vocal star was born, whose records would be bought song unheard, and whose influence might create a demand for the sheet music. Song plugging increasingly centered on the recording process. It became important that a song was recorded with a vocalist and musical backing likely to please audiences. The recorded sound became an important dimension of popular music, although the physical limitations of early records restricted songwriters from even experimenting with musical forms that would not fit onto the standard single 78-rpm record.

Side-by-side with the music publisher, individuals making decisions about what was to be recorded by whom (later known as the A-and-R men [Artist and Repertory]) wielded thier influence over popular music. Phonographs now were to challenge the piano for a prominent place in the social life of homes and bars, and to exert profound influences on music education, and on the quantity and quality of American instrumentalists and musical literacy. One could have music in the home, of a validated quality, performed by a star, without having to invest the time and expense (and inconvenience) to learn to play an instrument. The modus of record promotion changed once the air waves could bring the sounds of music into the homes and automobiles of America. With the rare exception of the call-in request-program format, Americans would only have the negative veto control over what they would hear by changing the station or turning the set off. The formative role of radio broadcasting over what music was to be popular music in America is well illustrated by changes brought by the ASCAP strike of 1941. ASCAP had acted as intermediary between the broadcasting stations and the copyright holders for the collection of performance royalties. When negotiations for new terms failed, music licensed through ASCAP could not be played on the air. ASCAP thought that it was negotiating from a strong position, since it offered a previously unchallenged catalogue of popular and other music of established publishers. At this point Broadcast Music Incorporated (B.M.I.) entered the field as a competing organization of publishers and songwriters not represented by ASCAP. BMI worked with many composers around the country, and when stations turned to BMI, programming became augmented beyond the previously urban, largely New York-based music. Music from the South and the West, recorded in Nashville and other places, made its appearance on national radio, promoted by recording companies outside the previously restricted regions.

Once the ASCAP strike was settled, side-by-side with old standards could now be heard the regionally based popular tunes. Many of these display close links to indigenous ethnic traditions. Even the urban dweller could now become aware of these when spinning the dial. And if sales figures of music in regional styles are any indication, there must be many followers of such music outside their regions. This is well documented in a series of papers by Peter Hesbacher and his associates for the metropolitan area of Philadelphia. In one study they conclude: "Since listener attraction is contingent upon radio programming, this factor was examined in three parts: announcing style, engineering-signal reception, and sound format. For the Philadelphia metropolitan area, sound format proved to be the most critical factor for attracting [an] audience. Moreover, the success of any one format is conditioned by the market's listening traditions and the formats being aired by other stations in the market."[4]

By sound format they mean categories derived from a three-part audial assessment—compositional structure, musical arrangement, and vocal interpretation—that generate a measure called *song type*. For the Philadelphia area they find ten song-type categories aggregated into either "mainstream": rock upbeat, pop upbeat, pop ballad, and rock ballad; or into "substream": folk, country and western, rhythm and blues, jazz, comedy/novelty, and seasonal music.[5] They suggest: "If the three-stage theory of social change and media growth is correct, communication through commercial radio will be more successful if it is directed to more homogeneous audiences, large enough for the station to sustain a profit and small enough to generate loyal listenership."[6]

Portable tape recorders for home use make the preservation of sound independent of studio-type recording gear and freed from the fixed duration of the 78- (or 45-) rpm record. With portable recording and playback machines, songs could now be "shown" to publishers, recording-company executives, or musical performers on a "demo' tape" (demonstration) without first having to write down the music and notate a lead-sheet.

Music that did not fit the 32-bar AABA format and followed a longer (such as the blues) or even an open structure (such as much of rock and roll) was now gaining the attention of decision makers in the music business. Regional artists could take their demonstration tapes for a hearing by the A and R men, who, if they decided to merchandize the composition, might not even bother to have it notated. They would simply listen to the tape and develop their instrumental and harmonic treatment from this aural experience. Moreover, the long-playing record—developed for the classical market but soon introduced in the popular field—freed record producers from the time limitation of the old single records.

Frequency modulation (F.M.) began to supplement amplitude modulation (A.M.) radio broadcasting.

The music-trade press began listing popular songs by some of the designations adopted by Hesbacher and his associates on popularity charts. The very existence of the charts became an important aspect of the phenomenon of popular music, since high placement, and even mere placement, on a chart conveys some degree of aesthetic approval for the composition. By setting up different charts for various song types, the invidiousness of having to pit songs of different genres against each other was eliminated, and different publics among the great audience of popular music could each be reached by playing for them the top songs of the week's charts.

The current variety of designations in popular music points to the existence of specialized merchandizing efforts and audiences and implies a cultural pluralism. The boundaries between these musical styles are fluid, yet performers of one style tend not to perform in another. Detached musicological analysis has found it vexing to differentiate between related song types of the music business, and has even come up with conclusions directly opposite judgments found in the trade press.[7] Perhaps it is more the performers' life-styles and the industry's desire to reach different audiences that differentiates, for example, between "acid rock" and "hard rock" as forms of popular music?

There is hardly a question that these and other such terms refer to different areas of music merchandizing. Performing groups and individual stars are identified with age and ethnic groups, and what Doris Day is for some, Janis Joplin is for others. Anything done by the [Rolling] Stones would not do for the country-and-western audiences, nor would Chet Atkins's guitar playing appease an audience assembled for a road show of the Jefferson Starship. As it is in other fields of contemporary merchandizing, much of the success of a product depends on the packaging. Electronic amplification often is more telling than differences in musical composition. The similarity of rhythm, harmonic treatment, and melody in the Ravel orchestration of Musorgsky's *Pictures at an Exhibition* and its treatment by the group Emerson, Lake, and Palmer is obvious, yet the identity of cultural subgroups becomes associated with such quasi-cosmetic modifications of musicological structure.

A preferred marketing technique uses a star performer so as to identify the piece with a performance category and thus with an audience. The audience recognizes the performer and associates the music with the marketing category of the music business. In this manner a great many people can relate immediately with the music and with one another through the shared musical experience.

Popular music is not as much a musicological category as it is a sociological phenomenon: It is music of the people and only secondarily for musicologists. To get to the people it requires the technology of modern America and the resourcefulness of its business community. From what is offered, the American public adopt some selections, but they do not first consult with critical musical authorities. The categories they recognize may not be supported by distinctions based on scholarly canons, but they are real distinctions in the cultural life of America—not only for the merchants who use radio stations to reach specialized audiences with their advertising, but also for people who enjoy these musical styles and their star performers.

For a great many Americans, the death of Janis Joplin and the breakup of the Beatles were more significant events than the death of Toscanini, the dissolution of the NBC Symphony Orchestra, or the annual deficit of the Metropolitan Opera Company. For these Americans, popular music represents not only the music of our times, but also a medium through which they converse with one another, explain their life-styles to their elders, and incorporate idioms and musical elements from the experience of other Americans into their homes—though they might not be willing to share the schools of their children with the children of another ethnic group.

There can be little disagreement over the proposition that in numerical terms, however computed, popular music dominates American musical life. The majority of radio stations broadcast mostly popular music, most jukeboxes play hardly anything else, most recordings in most places where records are being sold are of popular music, most of the new compositions registered for copyrights are of the popular genre, most musical instruments are of types featured by popular star performers.

The annual Gold Record Awards by the Recording Industry Association of America (R.I.A.A.), too, suggests that popular music garners the largest share of the market. "Revenues from sales of phonograph records and prerecorded tapes went up by 9 percent in 1974, although unit sales were down 3 percent . . . .Revenues reach a record high of $2.2 billion for the year, compared to $2.017 in 1973. . . .Most of the loss [of unit sales] was in sales of single records. Long-playing album sales dropped. . .1.4 percent. Sales of tapes rose from 108 million in 1973 to 114 million in 1974, revenues rising from $581 million to $650 million. In 1974 a new high of 195 Gold Record Award certificates was issued by RIAA." These awards are for singles selling one million copies each; and for long-play albums and tapes with a minimum sales of 500,000 units, provided sales volume is not less than $1 million—based on one-third of the list price of the album or tape.[8] Popular music also provides most of the background for television and the movies. No wonder, then, that anthropologists describe this as the music of the American culture.

The unifying feature of popular music appears to be its simplistic structure derived, however, from a complex musical and social history of intertwined ethnic, religious, communal, nationalistic, and business traditions.

Lyrics are important for an understanding of the popular music of given times and places, and they illuminate the connection between songs that are characteristic of a given social group. Because lyrics are specific, they might lead us to overlook the fact that entire age cohorts of Americans are reared to the sounds of the same music, the popular music that conveys to a nation of over 220 million individuals a message of their being united, and yet gives them as individuals, and as members of individual groups, the realization that in all that uniformity individuality is valued and supported.

We note that in America there are no government-controlled radio stations or television programs as are found in most countries of Europe or the Socialist Soviet Republics; instead there is a broad palette of radio stations (1972: 7,489 commercial AM, FM, and Educational FM stations). There is not one government agency with approbation authority over our music. To compose a song and have it published and performed does not require an official stamp of approval or a school of music certification that one is a "composer."

American popular music combines the music of the people who came to form the country; it is able to sustain this integrative spirit and still kindle the creative energies of its people. America's popular music has its musical basis in the cultures of the world. Through modern technology this music is shared with the cultures of the world, and other people recognize themselves in it.

Notes

1. H. Wiley Hitchcock, Music in the United States: A Historical Introduction (Englewood Cliffs, N.J.: Prentice-Hall, 1969), p. 47-48.

2. Ibid., p. 95.

3. Ibid., p. 108.

4. Peter Hesbacher, Robert Rosenow, Bruce Anderson, and David Berger, "Radio Programming: Relating Ratings to Revenues in a Major Market," Popular Music and Society (1975): 11.

5. Peter Hesbacher, Robert Rosenow, Bruce Anderson, and David Berger, "Solo Female Vocalists," Popular Music and Society (1975): 7.

6. Peter Hesbacher, Nancy Clasby, Bruce Anderson, and David Berger, "Radio Programming: Relating Format to Audience in a Major Market," Journal of Communication (1976): 12.

7. Mantle Hood, The Ethnomusicologist (New York: McGraw-Hill, 1971), p. 18.

8. The World Almanac and Book of Facts (New York and Cleveland: Newspaper Enterprise Association, Inc., 1976), p. 556.

9. U.S. Bureau of the Census, Statistical Abstract of the United States, 94th ed. (Washington, D.C.: U.S.G.P.O., 1973).

Other References

Etzkorn, K. Peter. "Georg Simmel and the Sociology of Music." *Social Forces* 43, no. 1 (1964): 101-107.

_____. *Music and Society: The Later Writings of Paul Honigsheim.* New York: Wiley, 1973.

_____. "On Aesthetic Standards and Reference Groups of Popular Songwriters." *Sociological Inquiry* 36, no. 1 (1966): 39-47.

_____. "The Relationship between Musical and Social Patterns in American Popular Music." *Journal of Research in Music Education* 12 (1964): 279-86.

_____. "Social Context of Songwriting in the United States." *Ethnomusicology* 7, no. 2 (1963): 96-106.

_____. "Sociological Perspectives on 'Youth Music.' " Discussion paper for the International Music Day, World Music Week Conference, Ottawa, Canada, 1975.

Hesbacher, Peter; Clasby, Nancy; Clasby, H. Gerald; and Berger, David. "Some Female Vocalists: Some Shifts in Stature and Alterations in Song." Forthcoming.

9

Jazz as an Urban Music

Dan Morgenstern

Everyone who has had even the slightest contact with the music called *jazz* has heard the proposition that the music was born in New Orleans, came up the Mississippi to Chicago, and from there spread out to points East (notably New York), West, and North, eventually to cover the globe.

There is a bit of truth and a lot of oversimplification in this cliché of musical history, but it is no accident that jazz is focused on cities. There can be no doubt that jazz, that unique and uniquely American music, was born and bred in the environment of urban civilization.

In this, as it is in so many other ways, jazz is different from so-called folk music, which almost invariably is rural in nature and origin, and seldom survives transplanting. Jazz thrives in all climates and has in fact become the first known musical form with claims to universality. It is the music of our century, as future historians no doubt will agree.

In that sense, the music's birth in New Orleans (which, theories to the contrary notwithstanding, is a fact accepted by most knowledgeable scholars) was symbolic of its destiny. Prior to the rise of New York, New Orleans was the most cosmopolitan city in the United States, a place where strains from many cultures came together and were woven into a multiethnic tapestry. As far as music was concerned—and New Orleans was a most musical city—there were African, Caribbean, Spanish (and thus Moorish), French, Italian, German, Jewish, Irish, and of course Anglo-Saxon elements, all in close contact with each other.

Jazz, which was the invention of American blacks, is a post-emancipation phenomenon. Prior to the freeing of the slaves, much interesting music had been created by black Americans, both in the South and in the North, but none of it was jazz. There are many reasons for this, but the primary one, perhaps, is that, in the words of the great pianist and composer Thelonious Monk, "jazz and freedom go hand in hand." Jazz, in essence, is a music that pits the individual against the collective in a symbiotic relationship—a kind of democracy in microcosm—and without the slightest doubt an art that could have been created only in a atmosphere of freedom, actual or potential.

From a practical standpoint as well, jazz could not have arisen in the slave culture. It is an instrumental music first and foremost, and the music making of the slaves was generally restricted to song of one kind or another. Instruments that did exist were of the homemade variety: various percussion devices, and stringed instruments, for instance, the banjo. (Slaves who showed exceptional musical talent were sometimes given musical instruction, and performed for their masters, but the music that resulted was made for and at the pleasure of the listeners, not the players.)

Black music in the North, while more often instrumental, was further removed from African roots and strongly influenced by European models; in any case, jazz is indisputably a Southern creation.

Instruments became available to Southern blacks for the first time in significant quantities in the wake of the Civil War, in the form of discarded military band instruments. Coincidentally, the latter part of the nineteenth century became the heyday of brass-band music, which provided a model for the new owners of cornets, trombones, and clarinets.

In New Orleans, the Creoles, free people of color, had acquired a musical tradition of their own, strongly French in accent. They excelled in particular as woodwind players and teachers, providing a link between the European and African traditions. The newly converted instrumentalists, on the other hand, approached their horns without preconceived notions about what was "right" and what was "wrong," and in the process developed a whole new vocabulary on their chosen instruments, much closer to vocalized sound production than to sophisticated European techniques.

And then there was the rhythm. African in origin, spiced with Caribbean flavors, it was applied to everything danceable and marchable, and there was plenty of both forms of exercise in New Orleans. By the time the final decade of the nineteenth century was under way, the city had become famed for its many social and fraternal organizations, and not one worthy of its name was unable to field a band for any occasion calling for music.

Such an occasion, in New Orleans, could be anything from a parade (and while Mardi Gras culminates the parade season, there were many other reasons for marching, year around) or a dance, to a picnic (the shores of Lake Ponchartrain were favored) or even as mundane an occurrence as the opening of a store. And then there were the funeral parades. The custom of accompanying the deceased on the last journey from church to cemetery with a brass band playing solemn music had been imported from Mediterranean civilization (it can be observed to this day in Spanish and southern French towns and villages), but New Orleans blacks added a unique touch: On the way back home, the band would intone the bright and cheerful strains of a hymn or march, played with the infectious rhythm that was to become the jazz beat.

There were other cities, naturally, where black people were making a new kind of music. Ragtime, though primarily known as a pianistic form, was also performed by bands of various sizes, and ragtime developed primarily in Missouri, where its greatest composer, Texas-born Scott Joplin, had settled (first in Sedalia, then in St. Louis; the latter city became to ragtime what New Orleans was to jazz). Ragtime also was, in effect, a new rhythmic setting for familiar musical strains— marches, quadrilles, even waltzes and tangos. But ragtime was not jazz.

What happened in New Orleans was that another basic ingredient was added: the blues. The blues, no doubt, was rural in origin; and to this day, we distinguish between country and urban blues forms. While jazz styles take their names from cities, blues schools are named for Texas, the Mississippi delta, and other such regional origins. Originally a vocal music, it eventually was accompanied by guitar or other instruments. The blues, to speak metaphysically, gave the soul to jazz, for the blues is a music of profound emotional quality, something relatively lacking in ragtime and marching-band music. The blues was the secular counterpart of the deeply moving music made in the black churches, of which the rather polite spirituals presented to white audiences were but a pale reflection.

The first, probably, to effectively meld the blues and ragtime, was a New Orleans cornetist and bandleader named Buddy Bolden, founder of the dynasty of trumpet "kings" that included Freddie Keppard and King Oliver, and culminated in Louis Armstrong. Bolden's career came to an end when he went insane (he suffered from paresis), and the story goes that he was seized by a fit of madness while leading his band in a Mardi Gras parade.

It was New Orleans, too, that provided the forum for interaction between blacks and whites without which jazz could not have spread its message so quickly and effectively. The city was relatively free from race prejudice in its crudest forms—another salutary effect of its cosmopolitan culture—and there was a good deal of easy contact between the races. In music, the light-skinned Creoles had begun "passing" into white bands early on; in any event, their approach to music was already quite Europeanized. By the early 1900s, a number of white bands were playing jazz in New Orleans. A black orchestra, the Original Creole Band (which had in its ranks the great Freddie Keppard), played in New York as early as 1912 and again in 1915; but it was a white New Orleans group—the Original Dixieland Jass (sic) Band—that effectively introduced the new music to the big city and became the first authentic jazz band to make phonograph records.

This authenticity, of course, is established in retrospect. But though W. C. Handy's black orchestra from Memphis was billed as a jazz band and recorded in the same year (1917), and James Reese Europe's black ensemble from New York had recorded as early as 1913, their music (and that of other contemporaries, black and white) bears less of a resemblance to what we now understand jazz to be than does the music of the Original Dixieland Jass Band. This is the sort of evidence that provides a factual basis for New Orleans's claim to be the birthplace of this music.

Another purported fact pertaining to New Orleans and jazz turns out to be pure myth, however. This is the hoary tale concerning the closing of the city's red-light district, which ostensibly threw so many jazz musicians out of work that they had no choice but to migrate to Chicago. Celebrated in fiction and film, this exodus never took place, for the simple reason that the houses of ill repute (which in New Orleans ranged from rude hovels to elegant palazzos) did not employ jazz bands. Some did have piano players (among the graduates of such jobs was the illustrious Jelly Roll Morton), and the fanciest ones had string trios; but the average jazz band of the day would have been much too noisy for the ambiance cultivated in such places.

At any rate, the migration of New Orleans musicians to points north had begun long before Storyville was closed by order of the Secretary of the Navy in 1917. The year 1912 marked the arrival in Chicago of Charles Elgar, a New Orleanian later to become one of the Windy City's most successful bandleaders and theater conductors, and head of the black local of the musician's union. By 1915 many New Orleans bands, black and white, were active in Chicago. Indeed, it was in this city that the term jazz, then spelled "jass," was first publicly applied to the new music. In New Orleans, if it was labeled anything, it was still ragtime or simply dance music.

The application began at Lamb's Café, where a band led by the white New Orleans trombonist Tom Brown held forth. Conservative dance musicians, fearful of competition from players whose idiom they could not (or would not) grasp, had thrown the obscurely indecent term jass at the invaders as a term of opprobrium, but Brown picked it up, wore it as a badge of honor, and flung it back in the faces of the disparagers.

The migration of jazz musicians was of course part and parcel of the general movement northward of a large population of Southern workers, black and white, in search of better wages and a better life. When World War I further spurred the demand for labor in the industrial centers of the North, the flow increased.

As an indication, the black population of Chicago rose from 40,000 (two percent) in 1910 to more than 100,000 (four percent) in 1920.

Other factors cemented the already close relationship between jazz and urban life. The national dance craze, which had begun with the cakewalk and spread through the ragtime years, gained momentum with the introduction of the fox-trot and other socially revolutionizing steps, chiefly through the efforts of the enormously popular dance team of Vernon and Irene Castle (whose favorite accompanists were James Reese Europe and his band). And in 1919, before the social mores shaken up by the war could settle down once again, came the enactment of the Volstead Act, with an impact that was nation-wide, but which hit the cities the hardest.

Prohibition and jazz, unlike prostitution and jazz, had a close, cause-and-effect relationship. The inumerable speakeasies that sprang up in the cities provided employment for musicians, and jazz seemed to be the music best suited for the irreverent and youth-oriented times. (This might seem a redundant obser-vation since the 1920s are commonly known as *The Jazz Age*, but F. Scott Fitzgerald and others employing that phrase did not use the term *jazz* in the sense that we do here; to them, it was much less specific—the kind of usage that crowned Paul White-man "King of Jazz.")

In some of the public mind, however, jazz clearly stood for all the things that were wrong with the age, and the considerable resistance to and public outcry against jazz in the 1920s was quite similar to the invective launched against rock and roll a generation later. In both cases, there was an identification of the musics with big-city wickedness as opposed to traditional (and by implication rural) wholesomeness. A report by the Illinois Vigilance Association in 1921-22 found that jazz had caused the "downfall" of a thousand girls in Chicago alone. In that same year, the superintendent of schools in Kansas City, Missouri, warned a convocation of the state's teachers: "This nation has been fighting booze for a long time. I am just wondering whether jazz isn't going to have to be legislated against as well."

The gentleman was reckoning without the political boss of his own city, Tom Pendergast, under whose benign neglect of public morality Kansas City eventually developed a night life that even surpassed Chicago's, so far as work for jazz musicians was concerned.

While Chicago was flourishing as a jazz center in the twenties (the city drew to it musicians from all parts of the Middle West and beyond), Kansas City was relatively a musical backwater. The early recordings by the city's most prominent black band, Benny Moten's, show a style still marked by ragtime and vaudeville touches already discarded by the better Chicago bands. Rhythmically, however, Kansas City bands already had something special; a rolling kind of beat that could also be found in bands from St. Louis (The Missourians, for instance) and Ohio. And there was a strong blues tinge, brought in by the Southwestern musicians who often worked in Kansas City—the center of band routes for an entire region, for which it also served as a trading center for grain and cattle—and whom the musicians from that city often encountered when touring Oklahoma, Texas, and other states.

By 1932, when it made its greatest records, the Moten band, with such excellent musicians as Count Basie, Hot Lips Page, and Ben Webster aboard, had achieved a kind of rhythm that was the direct precursor of the terrific 4/4 swing for which Basie's own band would become famous some five years later, as well as a style of arrangements that was the antecedent of Basie's "riff" style. In other words, Kansas City style had been born.

One reason why we can trace the Moten band's development from 1924 to 1932 so well is that it made many records, and one of the reasons why it did was that it was based in a large metropolitan center. Without the medium of the phonograph, the history of jazz would no doubt have turned out quite differently. A music dependent on individual sound, phrasing, and invention, jazz could not and cannot be properly notated, and had to be heard to be learned. The tremendous influence Louis Armstrong had on the development of jazz in the twenties would not have been possible had he not made many records, which were assiduously studied by musicians everywhere.

Without this process of careful hearing and rehearing, without this still relatively new and revolutionizing method of carrying the actual sound of the music to even the smallest speck on the map by means of a mechanical procedure available to anyone with a few dollars to spare, jazz might well have remained a regional form of music. It certainly would not have become a major art in which the influence of individuals had almost unlimited impact.

But we must not forget that the twenties and thirties were decades in which live music still had a great formative role to play. It was an era when hundreds of bands crisscrossed the countryside, stopping at dance halls and ballrooms in Godknowswhere as well as in the big towns, spreading the message of a new music. However, any small-town musician inspired by hearing the bands passing through, and learning his craft from the study of records by Armstrong, Jelly Roll Morton, Bix Beiderbecke, or Duke Ellington, would have to leave home and go, if not to Kansas City or Chicago or New York, then at least to Dallas, Oklahoma City, or Los Angeles to make his way in jazz.

No matter where he might be, New York was his ultimate goal. Even the best Chicago musicians yearned to make it in the biggest town of them all. Once you had been recognized there, you could be sure of a good job anywhere in the country. Obversely, no matter how good a musician or a band might be, not having made it in or to New York could be a crucial handicap. A case in point is a band mentioned by every surviving musician who played with it as one of the best—perhaps the best—of the day: the 1929-30 edition of Speed Webb's Hoosier Melody Lads. A drummer from Peru, Indiana, Webb began his bandleading career in 1925 in Toledo. The band had a good local reputation and recorded in 1926 for Gennett, the leading company specializing in so-called territory bands (ensembles that worked regional band routes and did not make it to Chicago or New York, the major recording centers; Gennett's studios were in Richmond, Indiana). For some reason, the records were never released. In 1926, Webb took the band to California, remaining there for several years and becoming a favorite with the movie colony. Webb's was the first black band to work in sound films. In 1929, he returned to the Middle West and formed a new band in Indianapolis. It included Roy Eldridge among the trumpets, Vic Dickenson among the trombones, and had Teddy Wilson on piano. The other trombonist was Teddy's brother Gus, one of the most gifted arrangers of his day. No fewer than six members of the band wrote arrangements, and this fact, along with its strong soloists, gave it unusual variety and interest. But though he had several offers, Webb was reluctant to go to New York, and the band, which made no records, never established itself nationally.

By 1930, of course, the great Depression had seriously affected the record industry. In 1928, well over 100 million records were turned out, while the figure for 1931 was just two-and-a-half million discs. Jazz—and especially black jazz— suffered the most from this decline.

That it was possible for bands from cities of no great significance to make it big is proven by two excellent orchestras from the unlikely spawning ground of Springfield, Ohio. Among the unresolved mysteries of jazz is how this city came to be the point of origin not only for McKinney's Cotton Pickers—among the top bands of the twenties—but also for Lloyd and Cecil Scott's Bright Boys—an accomplished group that recorded for Victor, then the most prestigious of record companies, and played long engagements in New York. And how was it that Springfield also came to be the birthplace of such distinguished individual talents as trombonist Quentin (Butter) Jackson, saxophonists Garvin Bushell and Earle Warren, pianists Don Frye and Sir Charles Thompson, and drummer O'Neil Spencer?

The Cotton Pickers, already a good band, rose to the heights when Don Redman, who made his reputation as Fletcher Henderson's chief arranger (and saxophonist-vocalist), became their musical director in 1927. The band's home stand by then was no longer Springfield, but Detroit, where they held forth at the Greystone Ballroom and were managed by Jean Goldkette, a French born erstwhile concert pianist who had come to the United States at the age of twelve. He organized a first-rate dance band in 1923 and eventually built it into what Rex Stewart, the Henderson and Ellington cornet star, has called the greatest white big band ever. At its peak, in 1926-27, the band included Bix Beiderbecke, Frank Trumbauer, Joe Venuti, Ed Lang, and other gifted jazzmen. The payroll of this star-studded ensemble became more than Goldkette could handle, and the band broke up, most of its members migrating en masse into Paul Whiteman's huge, high-salaried organization, thus giving Whiteman for the first time somewhat of a legitimate claim to his kingly jazz title.

The Goldkette crew often played opposite the Cotton Pickers at the Greystone, and on occasion interchanged personnel on recording dates; these were among the earliest instances of interracial recording in the annals of jazz. The music of these two bands, each in its own way, represents the best and most typical big-band jazz of the 1920s. Goldkette also managed, under its initial name of the Orange Blossoms, a cooperative band organized in Canada that would become the precursor of the Swing Era as the Casa Loma Orchestra. But Detroit neither housed nor produced any bands or musicians of national significance until more than twenty years later.

By then—the mid 1950s—it seemed that jazz had long since crystalized into an international art with no significant regional distinctions. Yet Detroit suddenly erupted with an unmatched outburst of native-born jazz talent, similar in impact to the Kansas City onslaught of the 1930s spearheaded by Count Basie, and carrying in its wake a young alto saxophonist named Charlie Parker. This was a new era of jazz; the age of bebop and beyond. A Detroit forerunner or two had been Milt Jackson, the great vibraharpist, and Lucky Thompson, the distinctive tenor saxophonist (who made their reputations in New York and Los Angeles, respectively.) But these two did not prepare the jazz world for the invasion of pianists Tommy Flanagan and Barry Harris, guitarist Kenny Burrell, trumpeter Donald Byrd, trombonist Curtis Fuller, bassist Doug Watkins, saxophonist J. R. Monterose and Pepper Adams, drummer Oliver Jackson, and three prodigiously gifted brothers from nearby Pontiac, Michigan: pianist Hank, trumpeter-arranger-composer Thad, and drummer Elvin Jones.

This outpouring was the last of its kind until the very different phenomenon of the gifted avant-garde players from Chicago's Association for the Advancement of Creative Musicians, who came to the fore in the late 1960s. Perhaps the Detroit flow was due to the fact that the city, as the seat of the automotive industry, had taken in the last huge wave of black migrants from the South in the days of World War II. One of the curious cultural results of this migration was the admixture of bebop, the most contemporary of jazz styles, with the music of the sanctified Baptist churches where the transplanted Southerners worshipped. In any event, the Detroit jazzmen combined a familiarity with all the devices of bebop with a profound feeling for the blues and gospel music—but then, so did Horace Silver from Norwalk, Connecticut!

By the mid-1940s regional styles, once dominant in jazz, had largely become a thing of the past. This was mainly owed to the impact of the phonograph record and of radio—the other chief medium for the dissemination of jazz, especially during the Swing Era, when bands broadcast from every major and many a minor hotel in the nation nightly. Another contributing factor was the magnetism of New York, to where every major figure in jazz had migrated, at least temporarily, by the turn of the thirties. It was in this city that a unique phenomenon, Swing Street, came into being in the wake of prohibition and maintained itself to the end of the forties.

Essentially, Swing Street was just one city block—Fifty-second Street from Fifth to Sixth Avenues—though it temporarily established beachheads one block farther to the west. At its peak, the "Street" had music behind almost every doorway, and one could hear dozens of the greatest jazz musicians in the world playing side by side nightly, inspiring each other and an entire generation of players and listeners.

That such a concentration of talent, made possible by the economic circumstances only a big city has to offer, should spawn an abundance of great music is no mystery; but who can explain why St. Louis is the hometown of so many brilliant trumpeters, from Dewey Jackson and Charlie Creath, through Joe Thomas and Harold Baker and Irving Randolph to Clark Terry and Miles Davis (from suburban Alton, Illinois)?

In any event, jazz, a music that has created its own sub-culture, a music that depends for its greatest achievements on the interaction between musicians of uncommon talent, and requires the support of a knowledgeable audience (an audience of the sort that only exists in sufficient numbers in a metro-politan community), is a music born in and nurtured by urban civilization.

Perhaps, as some social prophets would have it, we are now living in the twilight days of the big cities. Yet, despite urban decay and unrest, in recent years there has been an upsurge of jazz activity in our great cities. New York presently can boast of more live jazz, in clubs and concerts, than at any time since the 1950s, and New York still sets the pace. For the present, at least, the viability of jazz, the urban music, seems assured.

10

The Exhilarating Adventure of New Music in the U.S.A. since 1950

John Eaton

There was probably no time in history when it was as exciting to be a composer, performer, or auditor of new music as during the last thirty years in the United States! The dynamism, variety, and scope of new music in this country has been without parallel.

This is said with a cognizance of the many qualifications that must be made. The vast majority of Americans is totally uninterested and has been completely untouched by the new music. Yet the American composer addresses a larger audience than ever before—and potentially a larger one than ever imagined possible. Most American composers have no real functional place in society. In comparison even to their European contemporaries, few make a living from the music they create. Yet even if there have been more productive groups of artists in history, it is doubtful if any of them have ever had as much fun in their work. Zest, incredible activity, and a frequent feeling that they were crossing the frontiers into a different, more joyous state of music and of being—these essentials have characterized the musicians involved in new music in America in recent times.

Such was not the case in 1950. New music (we shall not discuss music that worked along lines already established by 1950, but rather that which works with materials, forms, and terms of communication not generally employed by composers before that year) was difficult to come by in the United States then. Very little new music was composed, and still less was performed and appreciated. In complete contrast to today, when they are extraordinarily active and prolific, composers of new music seemed to be dried up in 1950. They had little vital relationship with performers, and still less with an audience.

The change in environment and productivity since 1950 has been startling. What caused it? Although what we believe to be the seeds of dynamic changes were not actually present then, the soil was extremely fertile for two salient reasons.

Before and during World War II many of the most significant creative figures of Europe moved to the United States. Igor Stravinsky, Arnold Schoenberg, Béla Bartók, Darius Milhaud, and Paul Hindemith, to name a few, joined influential composers already settled here, such as Charles Ives, Edgar Varèse, Aaron Copland, and Roger Sessions. Each of these composers developed his own sphere of influence. Thus American music since the war, unlike that of Europe during the same period, has been characterized by many strong and divergent personalities and tendencies rather than a general style, despite a brief hegemony of Stravinskyian neoclassicism. Variety and a lively exchange of ideas became the defining mark of American music. Of course, with the pluralism of our national and ethnic origins and the sheer size of the country itself, it was virtually impossible for the kind of conformity to exist here as it did in the new music written in Western Europe, or at any rate performed there in the 1950s and 1960s, a conformity that impressed an outside observer as being rather like a yearly parade of fashion.

The other catalytic agent in the great creative explosion to come was our vernacular music, jazz. The influence of jazz on composers of formal music has been compelling and nearly ubiquitous in diverse and often-discussed ways. Briefly, our sensitivity to the individual rhythmic unit; our liking for downbeat rhythms and the frequency with which our phrases fall from the first attacks; the comparative ease with which we handle triplets, quintuplets, and other rhythmic tempi within the main tempo of the musical passage—indeed, our inclination to combine dif-

ferent metrical groups and tempi; our naturalness with syncopation; the weight that tone color carries in our scores; our
tendency to experiment with muting and other special effects;
the trust with which we allow more participation by the performers; our openness to experimentation with listening attitudes
and the degree of participation on the part of the audience;
the directness of personal, emotional expression in our music—
all these debatable points, and others, have been traced to the
influence that jazz has had on American composers. But this is
not what concerns us at the moment. Jazz gave American composers the possibility of participating in a living vernacular
tradition, of free experimentation and close contact with actual
living music making. This could not help but give us a vitality and
openness to new experience.

So that even though there was a general sterility in new
American music in 1950, there was an environment that could
produce flourishing vegetation if the right seeds were planted.

There were two polar tendencies available to our seemingly
effete American composer in the 1950s: he could court chance
or seek total organization. The leading representative of the
first tendency was John Cage, and of the second, Milton Babbitt.
It is almost impossible to exaggerate how much these two magnetic personalities dominated creative and conceptual thought
during this period. If you courted chance, you went to elaborate
lengths to divest yourself of any responsibility for the musical
results of a composition. But the musical results produced by
drawing the second tendency to its conclusion and determining
every aspect of a composition by predetermined number series
were not significantly different in actual sound from those produced by composers following the first tendency, as has been
pointed out by Rochberg, Krenek, and others. The composers who
sought total organization constructed tight networks; those who
courted chance wrote "idea" pieces. Either way new music was
difficult to come by: the per capita output was small.

In retrospect, I cannot help but see this first decade as a
formal and philosophical attempt to write with old materials by
extramusical procedures—as an end rather than a beginning.
(Neither Babbitt nor Cage produced disciples whose music was
half as interesting as that of their masters.) Radical composers
everywhere were forcing the forms, procedures, and even
criteria of other disciplines on music—in the case of the "chance"

composers, those aspects of the theater, literature, and the visual arts; in that of the "network" composers, those qualities of mathematics and physics. There was much thinking *about* music, little *in* music. Very few new compositions were produced, or heard.

What happened shortly thereafter seemed like an explosion: a burst on the world of music of a host of new musical materials and procedures. This was, of course, to some extent the result of composers working in the new trends of the 1950s, and more expressly of the activity of Cage and Babbitt themselves. But it was even more due to outsiders: technicians and creative performers.

The stimulus of vital new musical materials, which gave composers such exciting adventures during the 1960s, was brought about by two primary developments: 1) the democratization of electronic music; and 2) the discovery and common use of new instrumental and vocal and consequently new notational and ensemble techniques.

These two activities were by no means disconnected: they have, in fact, constantly cross-fertilized each other. The results coincided in another way: they were both bound to lead to the development of new pitch resources, and eventually to a new pitch orientation. Composers *in general* broke out from what an early pioneer on this frontier, Edgar Varèse, called the "prison cell of twelve bars." Electronic means brought about the easy availability of any frequency. It seemed to many composers a ridiculous hampering of the medium to remain with twelve pitches—even though several great works are both chromatic and electronic. At the same time, the attractiveness of many new instrumental colors depended to a large extent on their "out-of-tunedness" and the expressivity of many new vocal and instrumental techniques on their sensitive use of microtonal materials.

Let us consider first the democratization of electronic music. By the mid-1960s American composers for the most part had fairly easy access to the materials of electronic music. This was brought about largely by the development of small, compact, relatively inexpensive sound synthesizers. Large complex electronic sound studios were put into "suitcases" independently in the early 1960s by Robert Moog in Trumansburg, New York, Donald Buchla in San Francisco, and Paolo Ketoff in collaboration with composers at the American Academy in Rome. These synthesizers broadened the base of electronic music, turning it from an aristocratic amusement for a few elite among composers who had access to expensive, bulky, and difficult-to-manage equipment, to a vital part of the experience of nearly every American composer under thirty.

The postwar history of American music begins in earnest with the introduction of an iron oxide-coated magnetic tape in 1947.* At the same time that Pierre Schaeffer and Pierre Henry were developing "musique concret" in Paris, and Werner Meyer Eppler, Herbert Eimert, and Karlheinz Stockhausen were conceptualizing electro-acoustic music in Köln, Otto Luening and Vladimir Ussachevsky, two pioneers of tape music in New York in the early 1950s, recorded and manipulated musical materials performed on instruments, and then combined the final tapes with actual mechanical instruments played by live performers. This became, characteristically, a favorite procedure of American composers. The next generation of composers mixed all three approaches (the techniques of Paris, Köln, and New York) and their aesthetics indiscriminately. Within a few years no one even cared to differentiate between additive and subtractive synthesis over which so many inky battles had raged in the early formative years of tape music. This, along with so many other arguments from the beginnings of postwar electronic music, was a paper tiger. But the very existence of these arguments serves to underline how restricted the access was to electronic sound production in the 1950s and, by hindsight, how primitive and undeveloped were the means. The possession of the capacity to make an electronic music was limited to very few places opened only to a very few people. A handful of creative individuals were allowed access to the several studios that were in existence then. Few could even dream of utilizing "sophisticated" means, such as the RCA synthesizer. Even on this, four hours might be necessary to form a single note.

*The history of electronic music in America might begin at least with Thaddeus Cahill's Teilharmonium, which was invented around the turn of the century. It weighed seven tons and filled two railroad boxcars. From reliable reports, this monster could produce a fair imitation of a piano, a still highly difficult job for our most advanced means. Between Cahill and World War II there were many developments and much activity.

The first step toward making the materials of electronic music generally available took place in American universities, where many composers, in the sterile musical environment then, had fled in the 1950s. (Many of them, however, were not content to stay there. They formed contemporary music ensembles, which trained both performers and listeners and did much to create the vital situation we enjoy today.) Soon, with the aid of the Rockefeller and other foundations, many universities had classical tape studios. The means were still limited and expensive, and rather too difficult to manipulate, but at least the doors were beginning to open. Concerts of tape music became commonplace, as did the inclusion of tape-and-instrument pieces on ordinary concert programs. Still, in the early 1960s, before the invention of the small synthesizers, access to the materials of electronic music was very limited.

Another less restricted process was going on in the 1950s and early 1960s. This "outlaw" activity centered in New York around John Cage and might be called *live* electronic music. The central means here was the microphone, which was attached to instruments, a singer's throat, chairs, virtually anything that moved and made sound. The aesthetic goal was described as a search for the "music" of life itself. This part of the mannerism of the fifties prevented any substantial musical progress, but a lot of fascinating sound material was uncovered and explored as the "sound of life" was fed into various—often homemade—feedback, filtering, and modulating circuits.

The musical thought of John Cage and his associates, Morton Feldman and Earle Brown (possibly an unfair grouping) has had far more influence on new music in Europe than in America. Elliott Carter once suggested that this was because Europe has had fixed musical institutions that needed questioning, whereas we in America were trying to build institutions. One might also consider that in jazz Americans have a viable vernacular alternative to the attitudes and mechanism of formal music. The influence of Cage, et al. in this country had much more cultural impact than a purely musical one, but it would be difficult to overestimate Cage's influence on American composers. Perhaps his chief contribution in a purely musical way has been toward the liberation of sound, as evidenced in his live electronic music. By making us more aware of sounds as individual entities, he has stimulated the search for interesting sonic material. If

Webern made us aware of points of individual pitch, Cage—with Varèse—has been the primary influence in breaking up these pitch units into interesting colors, thereby setting the stage for the major subsequent development in musical materials.

The search for new sounds and for ways of handling electronic materials continued frantically. There was a general dissatisfaction in the late 1950s with the sounds of tape-recorder music, whatever the source. If they were generated purely electronically in those early years they were usually too simple to serve as the vehicles for a sophisticated musical train of thought. On the other hand, the musique concret sounds were frequently loaded with associations that went beyond and often destroyed the musical fabric of the work. Interesting sounds were sought in many ways; building special circuits for electronically producing and processing unique sonics was one of the most fruitful endeavors at that time. Its progeny includes the homemade instruments of Gordon Mumma and David Tudor, as well as enterprises as involved as Salvitore Martirano's "logic workshop" at the University of Illinois.

The dream of some was to utilize the most *sophisticated* electronic circuits of all, the ones in digital computers, to generate music.

In various ways, Max Matthews and later in the 1960s Godfrey Windham and James Randall at Bell Labs, Lejarin Hiller at the University of Illinois, and Pietro Grossi and Iannis Xenakis at Indiana University, and others at a host of American universities (of which Stanford undoubtedly stands out) addressed themselves to the problem of using computers to compose and perform music. Diderot, in his novel *Rameau's Nephew,* speaks of someone practicing finger exercises and unknowingly manipulating logarithms that would boggle the mind of a mathematician. This has been a problem of computer music: the mathematics of interesting musical sound alone are so complex that—with the exception of a few very large and sophisticated computers—unless the computer is placed at some distance from the production of music and given specific tasks to do, its circuits boggle.

Some of the more successful approaches have been using it to: 1) choose notes for (or scatter them to) traditional musical instruments, as witnessed in Xenakis's "stochastic" programs; 2) duplicate the operations of electronic-sound synthesizers or

extensions of them in a specific program (this is really all that
the computer program music IV does); 3) program other electronic-music apparatus; and 4) something so pedestrian as
copying the parts from a very traditional musical score.

Unfortunately little if any music has been generated so far
by the computer in the United States, which has an interesting
musical identity of its own. More and more, the technology of
digital computers has been miniaturized and incorporated in
other kinds of electronic instruments: dividers, sequencers, and
interfaces have been incorporated into most synthesizers
already. Soon the technology of most parts of all synthesizers
will be digital. Perhaps some more direct entry into a digital
computer will be devised—much work has been done in this
area already—that allows the composer to run, hear, and choose
more interesting sonic possibilities. Perhaps this is a prejudice
of ours, but unless a composer has direct, even physical contact
with his sonic material, not much progress will be made toward
giving computer music a real identity and personality.

But certainly we are at the beginning, and need to invent
and investigate *other* approaches. It seems as though we are at
a phase in computer music similar to that we have described
in electronic music in the 1950s: much theory, little actual music
making, and therefore little taste. And now computer facilities
are becoming more generally available. The major problem that
has plagued computer music is perhaps soon to be relieved as
that of electronic music has been by its democratization.

Small, relatively inexpensive sound synthesizers began
appearing in the mid-1960s and the means of electronic music
became generally available. At first the "suitcases" of Moog,
Buchla, and Ketoff were intended to make electronic-tape studio
equipment more readily available, but they were soon seen to
be instruments in embryo. The present writer used the Syn-Ket
in Rome in early 1965; Donald Erb, the Moog synthesizer in
Cleveland in late 1965 and in New York in early 1966; and Morton
Subotnik, the Buchla Box in San Francisco in late 1966. These
performances were all "live," without any prerecording. Soon
there were concerts using these synthesizers throughout the
United States. They were combined with chamber ensembles and
even symphony orchestras.

Now there are more than a dozen companies manufacturing
synthesizers in the United States. All of them are different—

almost all have some advantages over others, and each has drawbacks as well. Most of them, despite the real progress in the direction of live performance—built-in patches, touch-sensitive keyboards, preprogramming—remain cumbersome and somewhat unreliable and therefore useful only in conjunction with tape studios. Yet there are reasons to believe that electronic musical instruments will eventually be more refined and responsive to performers than mechanical ones.

One of the first things to occur to composers was to take advantage of the different character of different synthesizers (or different control devices plugged into the same computer rank) by specializing the role each instrument plays. The parallel with the symphony orchestra is obvious. Some instruments are struck—and this very human gesture of simply hauling off and whacking a percussion instrument was unfortunately lost in early electronic music. (Is there any less musical a gesture than turning a dial?) Other instruments are played on continuous boards or strings. Others have discrete degrees such as keyboards. All of these have their place in music making. Why not combine them? Toward the end of the 1960s, not only had many composers written for groups of synthesizers, but there were many groups employing improvisation and extemporization, such as Musica Elettronica Viva, which included at various times Frederic Rzewski, Allan Bryant, Alvin Curran, and Richard Teitelbaum, and the Sonic Arts Group, composed of Alvin Lucier, Gordon Mumma, David Behrman, Robert Ashley, and others.

But meanwhile, in the late 1960s, electronic music had become a vital part of the entire musical culture of the United States. This was mainly due to the development and general proliferation of the electronic sound synthesizer. By 1970, nearly every university had an electronic music studio; many high schools and even elementary schools had them as well. The synthesizer had permeated and enriched nearly every phase of our music. Background music for films and television—especially commercials—relied increasingly on them. Vernacular and commercial music such as jazz, rock, and country had begun to use these instruments with great gusto. Scarcely any composer under thirty could be found in the United States without some experience in electronic music. The democratization of electronic music had been accomplished.

Now we turn to the second primary, and parallel, development that gave composers the stimulus of vital new materials and made the music of our time an exciting adventure for all concerned: the discovery and common use of new instrumental, vocal, ensemble, and notational techniques. The general proliferation of electronic sounds that the democratization of electronic music brought about generated interest in their imitation both by vocal and instrumental performers or by composers writing for groups of traditional instruments. This is not to say that the discovery and common use of these new techniques was not well under way by the time electronic music had been democratized. But certainly the new means of producing music was a great stimulus to the imagination of all who were involved in creating new clothes from the older but still rich cloth.

Earlier in the century, the great laboratory of new instrumental techniques had been jazz. Singing and playing simultaneously, bending and glissing, flutter, and other special tonguing techniques, growling and other extraordinary ways of playing, double and even triple mutes to constantly and quickly change the color, and even multiphonics—all had been tried out by jazz players. Duke Ellington's band was especially innovative with regard to new techniques of performance both by individual soloists and groups of instrumentalists. But it was not until the early 1960s that soloists appeared in formal music with well-controlled and expressively developed new techniques as the cornerstones of their playing.

The first performer really to develop systematic and reliable controls over multiphonics and the other emerging instrumental techniques in an expressive and musical way was the clarinetist William O. Smith. This remarkable performer and composer commanded over 750 multiphonics, as well as many new types of trills and glissandi. In his hand the clarinet became, in sonic effect, a portable electronic-music laboratory and much more. The sounds he produced were much more colorful, complex, and personally controlled than the ones finding their way from loud speakers in this period.

No less remarkable, and soon to lead a revolution in string playing, was the contrabass virtuoso Bertran Turetsky. He was, unfortunately, not a composer, but he was a determined commissioner. He pulled about 150 innovative bass pieces from composers, making it the most written-for solo string instrument of the 1960s. He gave the bass a new personality of its own and in so doing expanded the pizzicato and coloristic possibilities of all stringed instruments.

The innards of the piano had been strummed and plucked by Henry Cowell in the 1920s and turned into a colorful percussion ensemble by the preparations of John Cage in the 1940s. But now pianists and composers began developing special techniques of playing on the strings with particular materials to produce specific microtonal pitches and exquisite colors.

A host of remarkable singers appeared at the same time. Like the instrumentalists they began by pushing traditional technique as far as it would go and by extending their ranges. They also adopted vocal styles from other musical traditions: Far and Middle Eastern musics, jazz, yodeling, and the folk musics of the world. Then new ways of coloring sound with the voice began to be developed, often in imitation of electronic music.

Eventually there were outstanding performers extending the possibilities of every instrument. It was natural for the new performers to get together and play in ensemble, especially considering the fact of their frequently having had experience with jazz. Improvisation groups were the color laboratories of the 1960s. Nearly every coloristic technique found in the electrifying and electrified scores of a few years later were first tried in these ensembles. Sometimes their playing was little more than dabbling in a frantic search for new colors: at other times it opened new vistas in musical communication as well, but always it stimulated the composers among them. After a time, however, all this activity in improvisation dwindled to nothing. The groups simply batted around meaningless clichés, once the exploring was done. No real vernacular tradition was formed.

These same improvisation groups processed their sounds electronically and hosted performers on synthesizers or composers with tapes. Conversations ensued among electronic, vocal, and instrumental musicians in which it was often impossible to tell who was speaking. Many borrowings from other musical traditions soon found their way into these ensembles. The culmination of this development in one direction was possibly the founding of the World Band by Richard Teitelbaum in the late 1960s, in which practically every player came from a different improvisatory tradition. Improvisers and composers such as George Crumb felt free not only to use snatches of sound or melodies from other musics, but also to evoke the words of these musics. Drones conjuring up the philosophy of the East if not its music became a regular feature in many scores, and similarly, in the late 1960s Terry Riley, Philip Glass, Steven Reich, and various other composers began experimenting with long hypnotic repetitions of minimal musical materials.

At the same time that solo performance was being revolutionized in and around improvisation ensembles, American composers were experimenting with innovations in handling groups of musicians. This activity became very much influenced by extemporisational and improvisational* techniques and ideas and the experience of working with them. All degrees of both were tried. Freedom was given to performers to choose particular materials in the moment of execution. Performers or conductors were to order blocks of material in such works as Earle Brown's *Available Forms*. (We have a feeling that American composers have generally been less involved with form as a schematic or mold than with what happens to material as it is played with.) Although the lead in aleatoric music passed to Poland with its state-supported orchestras simply because American composers could not experiment adequately with aleatoric devices within the framework of our unionized organizations, American composers continued to work extensively in aleatoric modes. Proportional notation was widely used in the early 1960s and became a general device by the middle of the decade. Conductors became cuers rather than time beaters, since time was left open to be filled by similarly unmeasured sonic events. These portions with no tempi were combined with others with multiple tempi (and conductors) in the same piece.

*Extemporisation attempts to break completely free from any shared context of music making by the use of chance techniques and other methods that try to avoid personal control by the ears and taste of the music makers. This is, finally, a philosophical goal and not an aesthetic one. Improvisation, on the other hand, employs, if not a vernacular tradition, at least a shared community of sonic ideas. The boundaries between the two are in practice hazy and indefinite. What the improvisation groups used in the 1960s was often some combination of the two. Likewise, composers were to use and invent techniques and notations that would involve both areas of activity.

By the late 1960s the new aleatoric techniques of notation and ensemble performance predominated in at least sixty percent of all scores of new music written by Americans under thirty. Inevitably, people became tired of the sound and the fury of the dense, event-filled aleatoric manner, which too often signified almost nothing. It was inevitable that there would begin a new search for the exquisitely wrought gesture, the sensitively evocative phrase.

But before we turn to the period of consolidation, the third period in new American music since 1950 as we are outlining it—in which the new materials exploded in the second period are being absorbed into a highly personal language by the composers using them—we must look briefly at some new developments in performance.

All but a few composers before 1960 were content to present their music in concerts, where a public simply watched the performers, who were supposed to dress formally and act simply, if not rigidly. Perhaps the *reductio ad nauseam* of this was the classic electronic-tape concert, in which a well-dressed audience sat before a few well-draped and unmoving loud speakers.

The situation was aggravated by the omnipresence of recordings. While it is difficult to exaggerate the importance of records in propagating new music—there are almost no mature composers who do not have recordings of their works these days—there are serious drawbacks. The liveliness of true sound is seriously curtailed, first by putting a performer on tape, then by compressing the sound of that tape onto a record. Watching a performer's gestures is often the best indication of the human content of the music he is playing. If music performances grew generically from ritual, and to a large extent they did, is not something lost when a listener does not join with others even in the last remnants of an earlier ceremony?

But for many composers these last remnants were simply not enough. In the 1960s they began in earnest to include something interesting to see as well as hear in their pieces. While many of the earlier "mixed" works were written by composers who were not very sophisticated in terms of the theater, and the visual part is often downright distracting or even silly; nevertheless, concerts suddenly came to life again, and attendances jumped. Performers are unfortunately not always the best actors either, but they were suddenly having fun again.

Perhaps the strongest single impulse to liven up a concert with "visuals" was the availability of these "visuals": easily controlled lighting; inexpensive, movable slide projectors; readily available strobe lights; and, above all—since most of the early mixed and multimedia experiences took place in universities (particularly outstanding was the Once Group of the University of Michigan)—the existence of theater, dance, radio, television, art, film, and audiovisual departments, members of which were ready and able to get into the act.

By the late 1960s there were mixed and multimedia events everywhere in the United States. Very soon much of this activity was supported by and found its way into the rock scene. Tributaries flowed into opera, film, and television as well. But concerts were never to be the same.

If only there were some way to convey a feeling of the enormous and feverish activity that characterized new music in the United States in the 1960s! Everywhere composers were spinning off ideas and pieces. Every day seemed to bring a "major breakthrough," a "thrilling discovery!"

We see the period since 1950 in three stages that coincide approximately with the decadal subdivisions:

1) First decade—a formal and philosophical attempt to work with old materials by extramusical procedures. Little music was written, less performed, still less appreciated.

2) Second decade—A burst on the musical scene of a host of new materials and procedures that we have tried to organize under the two categories mentioned above. There was extensive and intensive activity and a large and vital audience came into being for the new music.

3) Our own period since about 1970. The new techniques have slowly been absorbed by the sensibilities of composers. This process has been accompanied by the general adoption of expanded tuning systems and new notational procedures. There is a search for the exquisitely wrought gesture, the sensitively evocative phrase, accompanied by careful cultivation and even weeding out.

A description of this third phase will be even more conjectural than that of our first two. Now we are in our own time, and a description of it necessarily involves a projection into the future. There are only two things we can say about the music of the future: 1) It has not happened yet; and 2) there will be some if there are human beings. The making of music is a basic human need—at least as necessary to us as it is to birds, whales, or wolves. All human music springs from this simple urge to "sing." And because of this we are willing to stick our heads in the noose, describing the 1970s and attempting to project the immediate future.

In the 1970s open human expression has come into the forefront of musical experience again, although its tone is perhaps deeper and more mystical than before. There is both a feeling of consolidation and a freedom to cross aesthetic boundaries in American music today, of working in a sensitive and personal way with a new musical language. Composers everywhere in this country are opening up and honestly addressing their audiences in musical terms, using the new materials they have absorbed.

In much of the music being written, color, texture, and rhythm bear the main expressive weight. Pitches are mainly significant for what they do not do, rather than for what they do do. (We must except the obvious evocations of other musics or even older music of our own tradition from this general rule.)

It is a curious fact that in the musics of both our most interesting new orchestral composer, Donald Erb, and chamber music composer, George Crumb, earlier forms of pitch organization have been increasingly rejected. In their earlier works one feels that the systematization of pitch they use encumbers the flow of the music. But they are not simply "color" composers. Rather they are trusting the real composer's only ultimate tools: his ear and his musical intuition. We believe what is happening in their music is that a new flow is being born based on a different and expanded organization of pitch, a flow that would be halted by any too obvious a return to systematized chromaticism, for instance.

Intuitively and unsystematically, as is proper, these composers have entered the new microtonal world made available by the democratization of electronic music, with its ready availability of any frequency, and the new performance techniques, the attractiveness of which depends to a large extent on their "out-of-tunedness" and the sensitive use of microtonal materials.

The use of microtones is now general and their systematization has become a necessity. Perhaps the next big division among composers will be over which principle to use to organize the new microtonal domain—it has really already begun. Eventually, the desire for a rich and deep musical language will demand specific degrees in an expanded system of tuning. Briefly the two methods for deriving a new pitch organization are:

1) Create an entirely new scalar system from the upper partials of a note. This gives one the rather dubious advantage of pure intervals. It, however, makes anything approaching modulation difficult and cumbersome.

2) Divide the pitch organization we have into quarter tones, sixth tones, or even some smaller division. This preserves much of the tradition while giving composers new possibilities of relation and movement, and performers a challenging field of action in which they can bend intervals to purity any way when the needs of musical expression demand it.

Of course a third possibility, entirely feasible with the development of electronic music, is to use both of the two approaches, sometimes pure intervals, other times simple division.

A few closing thoughts: Composers and performers are closer together than they have been in years. There is a larger and more receptive audience for new music than ever in recent memory. In fact, considering that in past ages only a tiny percentage of the public was ever involved in formal music, composers today address the largest and most varied audience in music history. New pieces by major composers are now eagerly awaited throughout the world.

We believe that America's real contribution to the world's formal music began in earnest around 1950, although the groundwork had been laid by several great precursors. The history of music since then has been largely the history of American music.

Here are certainly some reasons why it has never been as exciting to be a composer as it is today. With the discovery of a host of new materials, the warm human relationship with performers, and the possibility of reaching people on many different levels, it is a joy to be involved in the new music.

11

American
Musical Theater

Mary Elaine Wallace

While some form of musical pageantry is native to every culture, music theater—whether it be opera, operetta, or musical comedy—has a definite history. Seldom in early America was there a theatrical event without some kind of music; but when the lyricists began writing texts with appeal to the new country, the airs they used were already well-known songs of European origin. Later when pantomimes and extravaganzas were introduced to American theater, they were patterned after their popular French counterparts. When opera houses were built in New York and San Francisco, and even in many small communities across the nation, they accommodated primarily European opera singers in European repertory. The Broadway musical, often considered uniquely American, had its roots in the traditional Viennese operetta. But American society, never content to rely exclusively on imported products, borrowed from Europe a heritage of music and theater, and used this to create its own peculiar musical theater activity.

Today in America, college, university, and conservatory opera workshops are training singing actors and actresses to perform anywhere in the world in almost any language. The

National Endowment for the Arts, many private foundations, and state arts councils are lending support to young artists and producing companies. Almost every high school gives an annual musical theater production, to the delight of parents and friends. The list of summer opera festivals ranges from the nearly fifty-year-old Chautauqua (New York) Opera Association to those summer companies enjoying their first season, and the number of summer-stock companies presenting musicals far exceeds the ones doing only drama. All this in a society where the box office cannot pay the way and where government support is so limited that wealthy patrons and university budgets are the main source of support.

Evidence of the exact date when musical theater was first experienced by American society is inconclusive. However, historians whose writings are readily accessible seem to agree that singers and "commedians" (as they were referred to on playbills of the time) immigrating to America in those first years probably performed, as early as 1732, the English ballad operas known to be in their repertory. By 1751 the ballad opera was prominent on the playbills of theaters in New York, Virginia, and Maryland. By this time music societies and performing companies were thriving despite attacks from outraged clergymen and moralists. The American musical theater was beginning its struggle for independence just as the country itself was yearning for freedom.

The most popular ballad opera of the times was John Gay's *The Beggar's Opera*, with its spoken dialogue and sixty-nine folk songs and airs. It had been premiered in England 9 February 1728, and performed a record-breaking sixty-two times in its first year. Its popularity and its claim to a place in the history of both opera and musicals is not difficult to understand. For all historical purposes it was one of the earliest successful operas; quite different, but no less successful, was Kurt Weill's twentieth-century adaptation of it, which we have come to know as the popular musical, *The Threepenny Opera*.

The Beggar's Opera appears again and again in the annals of early American theater until finally in May 1769, Dibdin's *The Padlock* and Samuel Arnold's *Maid of the Mill* were introduced to American audiences. *The Padlock* had successfully premiered in London only seven months before, indicating that word of this ballad opera's popularity spread quickly. Even though drama was still the main fare on American playbills, the 1769-70 season began with the addition of more ballad operas and pantomimes.

Little progress was recorded during the years of the American Revolution when Congress frowned on the extravagance of entertainments and, through prohibitive legislation, interrupted momentarily the momentum that had begun. Military officers who were willing to try the classic acting roles as a diversion during this time were not as confident when it came to singing opera. Records do show that some of the best musicians of the regimental bands were pressed into service in pit orchestras when such performances were given as charities. It may be assumed that the instrumental accompaniment was of finer quality than the amateur singing.

Following the Revolutionary War, the opponents of the stage continued to discourage theatrical productions, arguing that they had a corruptive influence on intellect and morals. Impresarios and managers disguised the performances by announcing them as "concerts with lectures," advertised to be both moral and entertaining. They even renamed some of their theaters and billed their mixed entertainments as *Spectaculum Vitae*, a term sufficiently baffling to satisfy their legal and moral opponents until the antitheater act of 1778 was repealed 2 March 1789. Thus the Old American Company, now with legal sanction, resumed its production of operas, musical farces, pantomimes, and ballads that were to develop and change with the maturity of the nation and the expansion of its musical culture.

During the last decade of the eighteenth century, more than 120 musical dramas of every conceivable type were introduced to American society. In 1796, there was a performance of a pantomime in two acts, *The Independence of America; or, "The Ever Memorable 4th of July, 1776,"* which, according to the opera annals supplied by Oscar Sonneck, began with an allegorical prologue and concluded with the Declaration of Independence and a country dance performed by the characters. French operas, so popular in Europe, found their way into the repertory at the end of the century, and Gretry's *Richard Coeur-de-Lion* was sung in English 31 May 1800 at the Park Theater in New York.

At the turn of the century in Europe, Paris was the undisputed capital of opera, while in America, English operas along with drama still held the stage. The swing toward Italian opera was just beginning. It is recorded that in 1819, an English adaptation of Rossini's *The Barber of Seville* was introduced to American audiences, and it is quite possible, though not confirmed, that Paisiello's *The Barber of Seville* had preceded this to the United States by several years.

The Park Theater was destroyed by fire at the close of the 1820 season and on its site was erected a new Park Theater that was to be the original home of Italian opera in the United States. The operas performed by the Garcia troupe in Italian during that first season, 1825-26, were *Il Barbiere di Siviglia, Tancredi, Il Turco in Italia, La Cenerentola,* and *Semiramide* by Rossini; *Don Giovanni* by Mozart; *L'Amante astuto* and *La Figlia del Aria* by Garcia.

The first New York theater built specifically for opera was called the Italian Opera House and opened on 18 November 1833, with a production of *La Gazza Ladra* by Rossini. Located at Church and Leonard Streets, it was to be the home of Italian opera for the next few years. In 1847, the Astor Place Opera House, a theater of architectural splendor, was built by 115 men of social prominence who guaranteed to support it for five years. On 10 April 1852, the Academy of Music was founded and dedicated not only to cultivating cultural taste by the entertainments that would be made available to the public, but also to furnishing facilities for instruction.

Many cities along the Eastern Seaboard including Boston; Philadelphia; Richmond, Fredricksburg, Petersburg, Norfolk, and Alexandria, Virginia; Charleston and Columbia, South Carolina; and New Bern and Wilmington, North Carolina, had theater seasons of drama and opera. New Orleans had the distinct honor of frequently being the first city in the United States to present opera in French; in fact, many times this French version was also the United States premiere of the opera. Between 1839 and 1843, such operas as Donizetti's *Anna Bolena, Lucia di Lammermoor, La Favorita,* and *La Fille du Régiment;* Meyerbeer's *Les Hugenots* and *Robert le Diable;* Bellini's *Beatrice di Tenda;* and Rossini's *Guillaume Tell* had all been introduced in French to New Orleans audiences. In 1851, San Francisco presented its first grand operas with performances in Italian of Verdi's *Ernani* and Bellini's *La Sonnambula,* after Chicago had heard *La Sonnambula* as its first opera on 29 July 1850.

As American impresarios struggled to outdo each other during the 1860s, men of wealth were planning new ventures designed to bring them social prestige. By 1880, the Vanderbilts and other newly rich, who had been unable to buy opera boxes at the Academy of Music at any price, solved their problem by financing a new opera house. The site chosen was the corner of Thirty-ninth and Broadway where the Metropolitan Opera House opened its doors for the first time on 22 October 1883. Although the social side of the Metropolitan Opera diminished somewhat after the gala opening, musical values rose with the appearances of such singers as Marcella Sembrich, Lilli Lehmann, and Emil Fischer during those first years.

During this same time of expanding frontiers and rapidly amassed fortunes, the musical theater that would eventually be "Broadway" to most Americans was also expanding. Still dependent on Europe for its more sophisticated musical entertainment, over eighty different operettas from Vienna, Paris, and London were offered during the last half of the nineteenth century. But along with these imports were the new American musicals. The 1866 production of *The Black Crook*, considered by most historians to be the first American musical, achieved unprecedented success in spite of strong disapproval by the clergy. A five-and-a-half-hour spectacle with elaborate scenery and lighting, and more than a hundred dancing girls, all exposing their legs, could scarcely go unnoticed.

In 1886 Victor Herbert came to America to play cello in the orchestra of the Metropolitan Opera House, where his wife had been engaged to sing. Within a few years he was to create a new style of operetta that was less complicated than its European models, and, in its simplicity, more American. The popularity of such operettas as *Babes in Toyland, Mlle. Modiste*, and *Naughty Marietta* were rivaled only by the operettas of Rudolf Friml, who came to America as a young man in 1901, and Sigmund Romberg, who arrived from Hungary in 1909.

And so it was in those years known affectionately as "the Gay Nineties," that Ernestine Schumann-Heink, Louise Homer, David Bispham, Marcel Journet, and Nellie Melba were drawing packed houses to the Metropolitan, with sometimes as many as a thousand standees, while Victor Herbert was helping establish the fame of three sopranos of unusual ability—Alice Nielsen, Fritzi Scheff, and Emma Tretini. By 1905, Miss Nielsen had deserted comic opera for grand opera, but Miss Scheff continued to be Victor Herbert's star performer.

Although men like John Philip Sousa and Reginald DeKoven were also successful practitioners of the operetta in the first decade of the twentieth century, George M. Cohan, a vaudeville song-and-dance man, was probably doing more to change the Broadway stage than any other person. While the composers of operetta concentrated on the music, the singers, and the orchestrations, Cohan capitalized on the speed and brashness of the new nation and its politics.

Many of Cohan's stage characters were based on actual people he had met or read about, and by starring himself in these roles, he gave the impression that he was the living incarnation of these people. Within a few years his creativeness wore thin, but to the American people his type of musical comedy—the fast-moving, breezy, dynamic, song-and-dance show—was fully established. The operettas with their beautiful melodies that had such appeal on Broadway and in open-air theaters across the nation, flourished side by side with the Cohan musicals during the twenties.

Jerome Kern's *Show Boat*, in 1927, marked another early milestone in American musicals. Its score and its lyrics by Hammerstein were among the best ever written, and its aim at being serious marked a crucial turning point in the history of American musical theater. The authenticity of background and atmosphere, the fresh and imaginative script also by Hammerstein, and the logical and believable love story made it a pioneer in the development of the musical play.

During the second decade of the twentieth century, the Metropolitan Opera briefly tried its hand at opera in English by presenting *The Pipe of Desire* by Frederick S. Converse as part of the 1910-11 season. It lasted only briefly, as did other American operas by Horatio Parker (*Mona*, 1911-12), Walter Damrosch (*Cyrano de Bergerac*, 1912-13), and Victor Herbert (*Madeleine*, 1913-14). By the 1914-15 season, the idea of an annual American opera premiere at the Metropolitan had been abandoned. Attempted occasionally after that time, it was not until the thirties that American operas achieved a degree of success. Deems Taylor's *Peter Ibbetson*, premiered in 1931, remained in the repertory for four seasons, but its sixteen performances represent a far shorter run than even some of the least popular Broadway shows. In 1933, Louis Gruenberg's *The Emperor Jones* received its world premiere at the Metropolitan. Lawrence Tibbett's spectacular impersonation of Brutus Jones at the world premiere was repeated in San Francisco in November of the same year.

Probably the most widely performed of all American operas is *Porgy and Bess* by George Gershwin, which first opened at Boston's Colonial Theater on 30 September 1935. Whether this is indeed an opera has been debated for many years, but its close resemblance to the traditional outline of grand opera and the size of its musical score with its recitatives, arias, and choruses, matches the grandest of operas. However, the American jazz texture of *Porgy and Bess* has been difficult for some musicians and critics to equate with the standard opera repertory without reservation.

It is interesting to speculate about ragtime composer Scott Joplin's opera, *Treemonisha*, written in 1911, almost twenty-five years before *Porgy and Bess*, but only recently orchestrated and staged. By the time it reached Broadway via the Houston Opera Company's 1975 production, the same question had been asked many times, "Is this really opera?" Joplin thought it was. Black singers and dancers have great empathy for the Joplin piece. Even though it depicts the blacks in Arkansas in 1887 as superstitious and uneducated, its message of "liberation through education" seems genuine when set to music by a black composer.

If the term *music theater* implies a marriage of music and drama, then only mention need be made of the vaudeville, revues, and follies, which were prevalent in the early twenties. The story line, if it existed at all, was feeble, and though a few songs have remained as popular hits of the period, they represent the composers more than the shows in which the songs were used. Revues and variety shows, when popular, have usually grown in size to extravaganzas only to diminish again when economic crises, or the rise of radio, movies, and television, or public boredom has dictated.

It would be unfair in any essay on musical theater to omit the musicals of Richard Rodgers and Oscar Hammerstein II, which are a solid part of our musical heritage. These men, along with their contemporaries, Alan Jay Lerner and Frederick Loewe, Frank Loesser, Meredith Willson, Bob Merrill, and others, gave us a new kind of Broadway musical in the 1940s and 1950s.

Romantic and comic figures alike were no longer presented as stereotypes but were human beings with whom the audience could easily relate. The musical numbers advanced the plot and the dances were an integral part of the action. These musical plays had a spontaneity and honesty that appealed to the American people just recovering from World War II. They flocked to Broadway and to theaters across the nation to enjoy the new musicals, which were not mere diversions but were truly emotional experiences. Original cast recordings that began with Decca's 78-rpm albums made the songs even greater hits as they reached into the living rooms of persons who had no opportunity to go to the theater.

Oklahoma!, *Carousel*, *South Pacific*, *The King and I*, *Flower Drum Song*, *The Sound of Music*, *Brigadoon*, *My Fair Lady*, *Camelot*, *The Most Happy Fella*, and *Carnival* are proof of the kind of musicals that were to sweep the United States and even go abroad as ambassadors of that all-American art form, the Broadway musical. Revivals, high-school productions, community theater performances, and summer-stock companies have kept these musicals on the boards for over a quarter of a century, breaking performance records over and over again.

Another kind of musical theater, the Broadway opera, developed in the 1930s. The already mentioned *Porgy and Bess* was an early example. Others were Oscar Hammerstein's *Carmen Jones* (based on Bizet's *Carmen*), Marc Blitzstein's *Regina* (based on Hellman's play *The Little Foxes*), and Kurt Weill's *Street Scene*, all of which had Broadway runs. In 1948, Benjamin Britten's *The Rape of Lucretia*, which has since returned to the opera house, came to the Ziegfeld Theater. Several Menotti operas saw successful Broadway runs—*The Medium*, *The Telephone*, *The Consul*, and *The Saint of Bleecker Street*. While Leonard Bernstein's *Candide* and *West Side Story* are more often included with musical comedy rather than opera repertory, the difficulty of the music and the size of the orchestra might easily classify them with other Broadway operas. It is this kind of musical theater tradition that has invaded our generation and promises to change the course of American-composed operas, making them more palatable to American audiences as they move further from imitation of European grand-opera style.

While the standard repertory of operas including works by Mozart, Wagner, Richard Strauss, Puccini, and Verdi continued at the Metropolitan Opera, only four operas were given their premieres there between 1935 and 1950: Damrosch's *The Man without a Country*, Richard Hageman's *Caponsacchi*, Menotti's *Island God*, and Bernard Rogers's *Warrior*, none of which remained in the repertory for any length of time. The next twenty-year period showed only four American opera premieres at the Metropolitan: *Vanessa* by Samuel Barber in 1958; *The Last Savage* by Menotti, which was given its American premiere in 1964; *Antony and Cleopatra*, Samuel Barber's opera, which opened the new Metropolitan Opera House in Lincoln Center in 1966; and *Mourning becomes Electra* by Marvin David Levy, in 1969. This is not a very exciting record for one of the world's most famous houses. Prominent companies such as the Chicago Lyric Opera, New Orleans Opera, and San Francisco Opera are, like the Metropolitan, basically traditional in their season offerings.

The New York City Opera, which had a full all-American season before it moved from its old location on Fifty-fifth Street to the New York State Theater in Lincoln Center, has premiered Copland's *The Tender Land*, 1954; Weisgall's *Six Characters in Search of an Author*, 1959; Ward's *The Crucible*, 1961; Moore's *Wings of the Dove*, 1961; Rorem's *Miss Julie*, 1965; Beeson's *Lizzie Borden*, 1965; and Menotti's *The Most Important Man*, 1971. Its repertory also includes Floyd's *Susannah*, Moore's *Carrie Nation*, and Hoiby's *Summer and Smoke*. Anyone who had the privilege of seeing the live telecast of City Opera's performance of *The Ballad of Baby Doe* had to be excited to know that this descendant of the Broadway opera had come into its own in the opera house and in the living rooms of television viewers everywhere.

During these same years, the Broadway musical was following closely the economic and social trends of the day. It moved from expensive sets and costumes for large-cast shows to small, bare-stage shows and back again with the rise and fall of the stock market. The Rodgers and Hammerstein years were followed by such hits as *Hello, Dolly!* in 1964 and *Mame* in 1966 (both by Jerry Herman), and then as youth rebelled against the establishment, the rock musicals *Hair* and *Your Own Thing* became popular. Composers of *Jesus Christ Superstar* and *Tommy* attached the name "rock opera" to their vehicles; the former found its way to Broadway, and producers of the latter rented the Metropolitan Opera House for performances there. In 1971, when a revival of *No, No, Nanette* became a Broadway hit, new shows were written to satisfy the craving for nostalgia. *Follies, Grease,* and *Sugar,* appearing in the 1970s, were each reminiscent of an earlier period, and *Naughty Marietta,* from 1910, and *Very Good, Eddie,* of 1915 vintage, were drawing crowds in 1976.

Broadway composers find their "angels" early, test their products in other cities before moving to New York, and even then cannot be sure of a hit. American composers vying for a permanent place in opera history must put down their pens long enough to search for commissions and grants that will support them while they write. They must find companies willing to premiere their works, and, even more important, they must hope for continued performance opportunities. Some, like Carlisle Floyd, have chosen the security of a professorship in a university. From Florida State University in Tallahassee, Floyd has seen his opera *Susannah* receive accolades from major companies and performed innumerable times by colleges and universities. His *Of Mice and Men* was premiered by the Seattle Opera in 1970 and *Bilby's Doll* had its first performance in Houston in 1976.

Dominick Argento, recent Pulitzer Prize winner, makes his home in Minneapolis, where he is on the faculty of the University of Minnesota. The Minnesota Opera Company is right there to premiere his new works. His *Postcard from Morocco* and *The Voyage of Edgar Allen Poe,* premiered in 1971 and 1976, respectively, are already finding their way into the American opera repertory.

Thomas Pasatieri is a prolific writer and can look forward to many more productions of his *Black Widow,* which premiered in Seattle in 1972; his *The Seagull,* first performed by the Houston Opera in 1974; and his *Ines de Castro,* premiered by the Baltimore Opera in 1976. He, like Argento, Floyd, and others, has written chamber operas that are being included in the seasons of college, university, and community opera.

Gian-Carlo Menotti has not been as successful recently as he was with the Broadway operas mentioned earlier, but his *Help! Help! the Globolinks!* received many performances in

American cities after its American premiere at the Santa Fe Opera in the summer of 1969. His most recent opera, *The Hero,* was first performed in Philadelphia during the Bicentennial celebration.

The visual consciousness of American audiences, heightened by the advent of television, has had a direct impact on musical theater. It has forced opera performers to be more than fine singers. It is conceivable that within a short time singers who cannot be visually and dramatically convincing will be acceptable on the operatic stage only if they possess phenomenal voices that cannot be duplicated by other singing actors. The American musical theater performer must train the body as well as the voice. After concentrated study in movement, acting, dance, and other related arts, the singer may be well qualified for dual performance in opera and musical comedy. The direction the singing actor's career will take is determined as the voice matures and the performance opportunities occur. A few, like Rosa Ponselle, Nelson Eddy, and Ezio Pinza, have been successful in both media.

For many years opera was limited to urban areas and available primarily to the socially wealthy. Television has demonstrated to the producers of opera and the agents of opera singers that if this art form is to become a true American commodity it must have the same exposure as other American products. So we find opera and musical comedy personalities appearing with movie, sports, and entertainment celebrities on the late-night talk shows. Short segments of musical comedies are programmed on television variety shows, giving audiences across the continent a preview of the musical before it reaches the nearest stage. A few full-length musicals have been seen on television, but in most cases the sale of movie rights prohibits successful Broadway shows from being presented on television before we find them on film, and years later in movie reruns.

A number of opera stories were made into films during the era of the silent movie, using at least portions of the musical scores by 1926, when the movies introduced sound. In 1930 *Pagliacci,* performed by the San Carlo Opera Company, became the first grand opera to be screened in its entirety, but the continued production of grand-opera movies in the United States is not impressive. Many operas filmed in foreign countries have found favor in the United States. The most recent and one of the most exciting of all opera films is Ingmar Bergman's 1975 movie of Mozart's *The Magic Flute.*

Opera in its complete, complex form has had some exposure on television. The Metropolitan Opera's presentation of Verdi's *Otello* on opening night, 29 November 1948, has the distinction of being the first grand-opera performance to be telecast from any operatic stage. The National Broadcasting Company and General Electric's television studio in Schenectady, New York, were the first to experiment with televised opera. Other United States commercial networks have on occasion promoted opera, but the greatest number have been produced by the British Broadcasting Corporation, the Canadian Broadcasting Corporation, and, in the United States, National Educational Television. Memorable productions of Verdi's *La Traviata*, Humperdinck's *Hansel and Gretel*, and Britten's *Peter Grimes*, to name but a few, have been tributes to the resources of both television and opera in the high quality of their production and staging. Some universities have experimented with televised opera, often with notable success.

The vitality of a live performance of music theater can in no way be duplicated through electronic means. However, the large sales of opera and musical comedy recordings are indicative of a listening audience with the inclinations and the advanced equipment necessary to support this market. When televised musical shows can be presented not only in "living color" but also in "living sound," American musical theater will benefit immensely. The cost of live telecasts of opera is now almost prohibitive, but with advanced technology these live telecasts may become as familiar as the Texaco radio broadcasts of the Metropolitan Opera that, since their inception in 1939, have delighted millions of Saturday afternoon listeners.

Producers, directors, composers, librettists, conductors, designers, and technicians involved in the production of American musical theater are an energetic, vital part of society. There is never a time when they can be less than pioneers seeking new territory for the outreach of musical theater productions; this journey into remote areas must be accomplished if the art form is to survive. There is never a time when they can be less than creative; American society demands the new, the different, the best. There is never a time when they can be less than shrewd business entrepreneurs; the American public must want the product and find the means to pay for it. There is never a time when they can give in to mediocre ideas or succumb to poor production quality if this marriage of music and drama—the American musical theater—is to survive and prosper. The enthusiasm and ingenuity of individuals dedicated to the promotion of this all-encompassing art form will not diminish as long as there is a song, a dance, a musically dramatic moment, or a "high C" to excite American audiences.

References

Brockway, Wallace, and Weinstock, Herbert. *The World of Opera*. New York: Pantheon Books, 1962.

Cone, John Frederick. *Oscar Hammerstein's Manhattan Opera Company*. Norman, Oklahoma: University of Oklahoma Press, 1966.

Eaton, Quaintance. *The Miracle of the Met*. New York: Meredith Press, 1968.

_____. *Opera Production I*. Minneapolis, Minn.: University of Minnesota Press, 1961.

_____. *Opera Production II*. Minneapolis, Minn.: University of Minnesota Press, 1974.

Engel, Lehman. *The American Musical Theater*. New York: Macmillan, 1967.

Graf, Herbert. *Opera for the People*. Minneapolis, Minn.: University of Minnesota Press, 1951.

Green, Stanley. *The World of Musical Comedy*. South Brunswick, N.J.: A. S. Barnes, 1968.

Grout, Donald Jay. *A Short History of Opera*. New York and London: Columbia University Press, 1966.

Krehbiel, Henry Edward. *Chapters of Opera*. New York: Henry Holt, 1909.

Lahee, Henry C. *Grand Opera in America*. Freeport, N.Y.: Books for Libraries Press, 1901, 1971.

Lubbock, Mark. *The Complete Book of Light Opera*. American section by David Ewen. London: Putnam, 1962.

Merkling, Frank; Freeman, John W.; and Fitzgerald, Gerald. *The Golden Horseshoe*. Edited by Frank Merkling. New York: Viking Press, 1965.

Rosenthal, Harold, and Warrack, John. *Concise Oxford Dictionary of Opera*. London: Oxford University Press, 1964.

Sonneck, Oscar G. *Early Opera in America*. New York: Benjamin Blow, 1963.

12

Musical Corporations
in America

Frank Peters

By musical corporations I mean entities that collect and pay out money, hire and fire employees, make contracts, own or rent real estate, and maintain a continuous institutional identity, all in direct connection with the performance of music before the public. These are chiefly the opera houses, symphony orchestras, and large conservatories. There is a great deal more than that to what may be called the music business. The fortunes of serious music in the marketplace are influenced by instrument-makers and concert managements, music publishers, performance-licensing organizations—such as Broadcast Music, Inc. and the American Society of Composers, Authors, and Publishers—music-rental libraries, record companies, studios and broadcasters, and local impresarios. But these are agencies that share the revenue of popular entertainment, live by their earnings, and can for the most part be readily supplanted, if they fail, by other entrepreneurs. The subject of attention here is the most prestigious and least profitable fraction of the musical enterprise.

The dependence of these corporations on subsidy is well known and requires little discussion here. A book by William

Baumol and William Bowen, *Performing Arts: The Economic Dilemma* (Twentieth Century Fund 1966) sets forth clearly the reason for the growing spread between earned income and expenses in serious music performance: Productivity cannot be increased by automation and the other means available to industry in general. A string quartet, in other words, is always going to take four players a certain amount of time to perform.

The nature of the musical corporations themselves has not been studied systematically. There are histories of a number of the major orchestras and of the Metropolitan Opera, but they are concerned chiefly with the record of performances, conductors, financial crises, audience growth, and shifts in artistic direction. Musical sociology is an academic field cultivated sporadically in the last century, mostly in Germany, but its practitioners—Max Weber, Theodor Adorno, Paul Honigsheim, Pitirim Sorokin, and Kurt Blaukopf, to name the best known of them—have been interested mainly in what kinds of music are composed in what kinds of society. Adorno saw that music had become something close to a market commodity over the last 200 years and tried to formulate the relation between composer and audience in the market. He studied the celebrated Society for Private Performances that Schoenberg directed in Vienna in the early 1920s. Adorno did not recognize an inherent conflict between the elitism implicit in such a solution and the Marxist ideal of a whole people in harmony with its arts.

Music taken as a commodity is not in trouble. There is an enormous amount of it at hand in the United States in the 1970s, serious and popular, sold on relatively cheap records and tape and broadcast free. Music comes out of loudspeakers, and pervades grocery stores, restaurants, and even parks. Music is such a thriving commodity that it is difficult to escape it. Almost everything Schoenberg composed can be reproduced at will in the music-lover's home, as often as he wants to hear it, in immaculate, clear performances, for an investment amounting to less than ten dollars per hour of recorded music.

It is the musical corporations that are in trouble. The Metropolitan Opera's financial embarrassment in the last few years has been well publicized, and at the time of this writing the Teatro alla Scala in Milan has declared its inability to fulfill its Bicentennial engagements in America because of the devaluation of Italian currency. Now the collapse or even retrench-

ment of these institutions is cause for dismay, but it is not
certain that their collapse would damage opera as an art, nor
impede the public's access to opera, live or recorded. There are
very few cases of actual collapse among major performing-arts
organizations on which to base a judgment. The hole left by
disbandment of the National Ballet in Washington in 1974 seems
to have been quickly filled, as far as the audience was concerned,
by the flow of visiting dance companies to Kennedy Center. The
symphony orchestras that have been obliged to break off operations have been reconstituted with changed boards and managements.

The question raised here is a sensitive and complex one:
to what extent do musical corporations serve themselves rather
than the public? If they fail, at whose expense is it—that of the
corporation's own directors, employees, and creditors, or that
of the musical consumer? In their absence, how readily can the
public find a substitute that is artistically satisfactory?

The answers to these questions would depend on particular
circumstances and would necessarily be speculative. Yet the case
for preserving the corporations against their rising deficit, and
for identifying their welfare with that of the arts, is forcefully
articulated by the employees of the corporation—administrators,
functionaries, and musicians—while only scattered voices
propose alternatives, and philistine indifference to the arts is
represented as the chief enemy of the beleaguered institutions.

While they maintained themselves as self-sufficient music
societies, supplementing box-office revenue with benefactions
from board members, their freedom of choice was beyond challenge; but in the last decade the large orchestras and opera
companies have come to depend increasingly on money from
public and quasi-public sources—appropriations from federal,
state, regional, and municipal governments, shares in united-
fund canvasses for the arts, and grants from tax-exempt foundations. All the twenty-nine major orchestras in the United States
have government revenue in six-figure amounts. It totaled nearly
$12 million in 1974-75. The biggest beneficiary was the St. Louis
Symphony, which in that year drew $1,023,000 from govern-
mental sources—$50,000 from the city, $139,000 from the
county, $629,000 from the state, and $140,000 from the federal
level, the remainder from miscellaneous public subsidies, such as
the regional Mid-America Arts Alliance.

All but $894,000 of the United States total for that year was paid for orchestral services. Public subsidy has not been a simple dole, and the money is not apportioned carelessly. Indeed, the scruples of the arts councils and foundations have obliged musical organizations to augment their administrative staffs (and expenses) in the devising of attractive proposals, gathering of data, filling out of applications, and accountancy for the whole complex financial apparatus. At the same time, the development of substantial government and foundation revenue has encouraged musicians to demand full-year employment and pay commensurate with their professional skills and their increasing per-week work load. To a great extent, therefore, public and quasi-public subsidy has consumed itself in increased administrative and labor costs, and the musical corporations have had to redouble their campaigns for philanthropic support.

The point here is not that public subsidy has been misused, but simply that it exists in a greater degree than most people realize, and that the public has acquired a substantial interest in the conduct of the musical corporations. In the St. Louis case, tax subsidy makes up about a fourth of the symphony orchestra's budget, or roughly $10,000 of the $40,000 it costs to keep each of 100 musicians playing for a year. Is it fitting employment of this large assembly of $40,000-per-year (reckoned not by wage but by the cost to society) artist-craftsmen to play "Turkey in the Straw" over loudspeakers in a park, to demonstrate instrumental sounds for schoolchildren, to accompany musical comedians at pop concerts, to play show tunes in an ice rink for a beer-and-pretzels audience? Could other musicians not do this work as well? Yet the subsidy system itself has thrust most of these functions on the elite minority of St. Louis musicians (100 out of 3,100 members of the union local) who constitute the St. Louis Symphony. At the same time the city lacks a professional dance company, is seeing the first attempts in seven years to reestablish a short season of opera productions, does not have a theater suitable for opera, ballet, and musical comedy, and neglects historic organs in music halls in danger of destruction.

Most public money for the arts is distributed by the arts councils that have grown up at various governmental levels since the middle 1960s. They are conscientious, but for the most part they react to the needs of the established musical organizations, weighing one application against another to determine the

apportionment of their money. Interested corporations can produce documented proposals, send out spokesmen, generate
publicity, cultivate politicians, and wield influence in proportion
to their budgets. To appeal to the democratic sensibilities of arts
councils, the corporations habitually propose audience-expanding
devices of the popular entertainment sort.

The arts councils can represent the public interest better.
They might employ investigators to determine the artistic needs
of the regions they serve, take initiatives, lobby in legislatures,
direct attention at areas in want, represent the public cultural
interest before unions, and in general serve music and the various
arts as assiduously as the established corporations serve themselves. A first step toward this goal would be a survey of the
extent to which arts-council board directorships overlap those of
beneficiary institutions.

Contributors

Kenneth B. Billups is assistant professor of music at the University of Missouri, St. Louis, and supervisor of vocal music for the St. Louis Public Schools. He is founder-director of the thirty-six-year-old Legend Singers, exponents of legendary black folk music. He is past president of the National Association of Negro Musicians, Inc.

Austin B. Caswell is associate professor of musicology at the School of Music, Indiana University. He is the translater of *Remarques Curieuses sur L'Art de Bien Chanter*, a 1668 singing treatise written at the court of Louis XIV by Benigne de Bacilly.

John Eaton began his professional career as pianist-leader of his own contemporary jazz group, with which he toured the country while a student at Princeton University. He has won three Prix de Rome, two Guggenheim grants, and other awards. As a widely known composer for electronic-music synthesizers, he has combined these instruments with live performers, and in other respects has sought to humanize the medium.

K. Peter Etzkorn is professor of sociology and anthropology at the University of Missouri, St. Louis, and visiting professor at Münster University. Dr. Etzkorn has contributed to scholarly publications in both English and German. He is the former editor of special publications for the Society for Ethnomusicology.

Charlotte J. Frisbie recently concluded a sabbatical from the anthropology department of Southern Illinois University, Edwardsville, for fieldwork as Weatherhead resident scholar at the School of American Research, Santa Fe, New Mexico. Dr. Frisbie is coeditor of *Oltay Tsoh: A Man and His Beliefs*, the biography of Frank Mitchell, a Navajo Blessingway singer. She is editor of the Society of Ethnomusicology newsletter.

Joseph C. Hickerson has been archivist of the Folklore Archives, the Library of Congress, since 1963. Previously, Dr. Hickerson was folklore archivist at Indiana University.

Edward Jablonski, a noted authority on George Gershwin, is a columnist for *Record Guide*. His articles have appeared in *Tin Pan Alley, The Saturday Review, Reporter, Musical America*, and theatrical publications.

George McCue is the former arts editor of the St. Louis *Post-Dispatch*. From 1956 until his retirement in 1975 he was the newspaper's art and urban-design critic.

Roy V. Magers is assistant professor of music at Winthrop College, Rock Hill, South Carolina. There Dr. Magers has continued Charles Ives research begun for his dissertation at Indiana University.

Dan Morgenstern, jazz historian, critic, consultant, and producer, was cofounder and editor of *Jazz* (later *Jazz and Pop*), and was editor-in-chief of *Down Beat*. He has written and lectured about jazz in many parts of the world, and is the author of the jazz entries in numerous encyclopedias, including *Recorded Anthology of American Music*. Morgenstern annotated more than 100 record albums for Columbia, RCA, and others, and won the 1973-74 Grammy Award for Best Album Notes. He is New York chapter governor of the National Academy of Recording Arts and Sciences. He has completed two books scheduled for publication this year.

Frank Peters, music editor of the St. Louis *Post-Dispatch*, won the Pulitzer Prize for distinguished criticism in 1972. Previously, he was managing editor of the Rome *Daily American*.

William Schuman is a foremost American composer of large-scale symphonic works, of string quartets, and of opera, chorus, band, and dance scores. He is the former president of Juilliard School of Music and of Lincoln Center, and is now chairman of the board for Videorecord Corporation of America. He recently completed a television series in New York on the subject, "What's American about American Music."

Mary Elaine Wallace, professor of music at Southern Illinois University, Carbondale, is the director of the Marjorie Lawrence Opera Theatre and its traveling troupe, Opera on Wheels. She was the first woman president of the National Opera Association. She has produced and directed thirty-two operas plus numerous musicals and operettas.

Indexes